Life Science
Grade Two
Table of Contents

We wake up in a new world every day. Our lives are caught in a whirlwind of change in which new wonders are constantly being discovered. Technology is carrying us headlong into the 21st century. How will our children keep pace? We must provide them with the tools necessary to go forth into the future. Those tools can be found in a sound science education. One guidepost to a good foundation in science is the *National Science Education Standards*. This book adheres to these standards. Another useful guide is the *Full Option Science System™ (FOSS). FOSS* focuses on insects and plants at this grade level—specifically, on comparing, communicating, and observing. The pages that correlate to FOSS are noted on page 5, along with the Curriculum Correlation.

Young children are naturally curious about science and life. They see the world around them and ask questions that naturally lead into the lessons that they will be taught in science. Science is exciting to children because it answers their questions about themselves and the world around them—their immediate world and their larger environment. A basic understanding of science boosts students' understanding of the world around them.

As children learn more about themselves and their world, they should be encouraged to notice the other living things that inhabit it. They should be aware of the differences between living and nonliving things. They should become aware of the interdependence of organisms—from plants, to animals, to humans. Children should also learn how they can control their own environments to promote their health. Through good personal hygiene, exercise, and making good, safe decisions while interacting with nature, children will learn how to take better care of themselves.

Organization
Life Science serves as a handy companion to the regular science curriculum. It is divided into four units: The Living World, Plants, Animals, and Health and Safety. Each unit contains concise background information on the unit's topics, as well as exercises and activities to reinforce students' knowledge and understanding of basic principles of science and the world around them.

- **The Living World:** Students learn what living things need to survive. They are encouraged to think about where different plants and animals come from, the differences between habitats, and what types of animals live in each habitat. They begin to form an understanding that plants and animals have adaptations that help them survive in their particular habitat. Students see how plants and animals depend upon each other and upon their environments. Students learn that they can harm or help the environment around them.

- **Plants:** Students learn about plants and what they need to survive. They learn about the different parts of a plant and the purpose of each part. They learn the differences between some plants. Students think about where plants live and learn how to grow a plant of their own.

- **Animals:** Students become aware of the differences among animals—mammals, reptiles, fish, birds, amphibians, and insects. They study the needs of animals and animal behaviors and adaptations that ensure that these needs are met. Students learn about the birth and care of young animals. Students are introduced to life cycles by putting together a project that shows the life cycle of a frog. Studying animals that have long been extinct and those that are in danger helps students understand the importance of taking care of the Earth.

- **Health and Safety:** Students explore the senses and how we use them every day.

Students learn about nutrition, exercise, and hazards in the home and their environments. They explore ways in which they can make good choices and find that they have control over their own health. They learn health and safety habits that they can develop and keep for life.

This book contains three types of pages:

- Concise background information is provided for each unit. These pages are intended for the teacher's use. The teacher or a helper may read some sections to the class.

- Exercises are included for use as tests or practice for the students. These pages are meant to be reproduced.

- Activity pages list the materials and steps necessary for students to complete a project. Questions for students to answer are also included on these pages as a type of performance assessment. As much as possible, these activities include most of the multiple intelligences so students can use their strengths to achieve a well-balanced learning style. These pages are also meant for reproduction for use by students.

Use
Life Science is designed for independent use by students who have been introduced to the skills and concepts described. This book is meant to supplement the regular science curriculum; it is not meant to replace it. Copies of the activities can be given to individuals, pairs of students, or small groups for completion. They may also be used as a center activity. If students are familiar with the content, the worksheets may also be used as homework. To begin, determine the implementation that fits your students' needs and your classroom structure. The following plan suggests a format for this implementation.

1. Explain the **purpose** of the worksheets to your students. Let them know that these activities will be fun as well as helpful.

2. Review the **mechanics** of how you want the students to work with the activities. Do you want them to work in groups? Are the activities for homework?

3. Decide how you would like to use the **assessments.** They can be given before and after a unit to determine progress, or only after a unit to assess how well the concepts have been learned.

4. Determine whether you will send the tests home or keep them in students' **portfolios.**

5. Introduce students to the **process** and the purpose of the activities. Go over the directions. Work with children when they have difficulty. Work only a few pages at a time to avoid pressure.

6. Do a **practice** activity together.

The Scientific Method
Students can be more productive if they have a simple procedure to use in their science work. The scientific method is such a procedure. It is detailed here, and a reproducible page for students is included on page 7.

1. **PROBLEM:** Identify a problem or question to investigate.
2. **HYPOTHESIS:** Tell what you think will be the result of your investigation or activity.
3. **EXPERIMENTATION:** Perform the investigation or activity.
4. **OBSERVATION:** Make observations, and take notes about what you observe.
5. **CONCLUSION:** Draw conclusions from what you have observed.
6. **COMPARISON:** Does your conclusion agree with your hypothesis? If so, you have shown that your hypothesis was correct. If not, you need to change your hypothesis.
7. **PRESENTATION:** Prepare a presentation or report to share your findings.
8. **RESOURCES:** Include a list of resources used. Students need to give credit to people or books they used to help them with their work.

Hands-On Experience

An understanding of science is best promoted by hands-on experience. *Life Science* provides a wide variety of activities for students. But students also need real-life exposure to their world. Playgrounds, parks, and vacant lots are handy study sites to observe many organisms. Repeated visits to the same site can help to show students that the organisms are constantly changing.

It is essential that students be given sufficient concrete examples of scientific concepts. Appropriate manipulatives can be bought or made from common everyday objects. Most of the activity pages can be completed with materials easily accessible to the students. Manipulatives that can be used to reinforce scientific skills are recommended on several of the activity pages.

Science Fair

Knowledge without application is wasted effort. Students should be encouraged to participate in their school science fair. To help facilitate this, each unit in *Life Science* ends with a page of science fair ideas and projects. Also, on page 8 is a chart that will help students to organize their science fair work.

To help students develop a viable project, you might consider these guidelines:

- Decide whether to do individual or group projects.

- Help students choose a topic that interests them and that is manageable. Make sure a project is appropriate for a student's grade level and ability. Otherwise, that student might become frustrated. This does not mean that you should discourage a student's scientific curiosity. However, some projects are just not appropriate. Be sure, too, that you are familiar with the school's science fair guidelines. Some schools, for example, do not allow glass or any electrical or flammable projects. An exhibit also is usually restricted to three or four feet of table space.

- Encourage students to develop questions and to talk about their questions in class.

- Help students to decide on one question or problem.

- Help students to design a logical process for developing the project. Stress that the acquisition of materials is an important part of the project. Some projects also require strict schedules, so students must be willing and able to carry through with the process.

- Remind students that the scientific method will help them to organize their thoughts and activities. Students should keep track of their resources used, whether they are people or print materials. Encourage students to use the Internet to do research on their project.

Additional Notes

- **Parent Communication:** Send the Letter to Parents home with students so that parents will know what to expect and how they can help their child.

- **Bulletin Board:** Display completed work to show student progress.

- **Portfolios:** You may want to maintain a portfolio of students' completed exercises and activities. This portfolio can help you in performance assessments.

- **Assessments:** There are Assessments for each unit at the beginning of the book. You can use the tests as diagnostic tools by administering them before children begin the activities. After children have completed each unit, let them retake the unit test to see the progress they have made.

- **Center Activities:** Use the worksheets as a center activity to give students the opportunity to work cooperatively.

- **Have fun:** Working with these activities can be fun as well as meaningful for you and your students.

Curriculum Area	Page Numbers
Social Studies	15, 19, 20, 21, 22, 23, 24, 27, 29, 30, 31, 61
Language Arts	15, 16, 17, 18, 19, 20, 21, 23, 24, 25, 26, 27, 28, 29, 30, 31, 32, 36, 37, 38, 39, 40, 41, 42, 43, 44, 45, 46, 51, 52, 55, 56, 57, 59, 60, 61, 62, 63, 64, 65, 69, 70, 71, 72, 75, 76, 77, 78, 79, 80, 81, 82, 83, 85, 86, 87, 88, 89, 90, 91, 92, 95, 96, 97, 98, 99, 100, 107, 112, 114, 115, 117, 118, 119, 121, 122, 123, 124
Math	27, 28, 64, 72, 80, 90, 91, 92, 114, 115
Physical Education/ Health & Safety	41, 50, 105, 106, 107, 108, 109, 110, 111, 112, 113, 114, 115, 116, 117, 118, 119, 120, 121, 122, 123, 124, 125
Art	17, 18, 21, 25, 26, 29, 31, 32, 36, 42, 43, 45, 52, 58, 61, 62, 63, 70, 71, 73, 75, 76, 79, 82, 85, 86, 89, 95, 96, 99, 105, 113, 116, 120, 125

FOSS Correlation

The Full Option Science System™ (FOSS) was developed at the University of California at Berkeley. It is a coordinated science curriculum organized into four categories: Life Science; Physical Science; Earth Science; and Scientific Reasoning and Technology. Under each category are various modules that span two grade levels. The modules for this grade level are highlighted in the chart below.

Insects	90, 91, 92, 93
New Plants	36, 37, 38, 39, 40, 41, 42, 43, 44, 45, 46, 47, 48, 49, 50, 51, 52, 53, 54, 55, 56, 57, 58, 59, 60, 61, 62, 63, 64

Dear Parent,

During this school year, our class will be using an activity book to reinforce the science skills that we are learning. By working together, we can be sure that your child not only masters these science skills but also becomes confident in his or her abilities.

From time to time, I may send home activity sheets. To help your child, please consider the following suggestions:

- Provide a quiet place to work.
- Go over the directions together.
- Help your child to obtain any materials that might be needed.
- Encourage your child to do his or her best.
- Check the activity when it is complete.
- Discuss the basic science ideas associated with the activity.

Help your child to maintain a positive attitude about the activities. Let your child know that each lesson provides an opportunity to have fun and to learn more about the world around us. Above all, enjoy this time you spend with your child. As your child's science skills develop, he or she will appreciate your support.

Thank you for your help.

Cordially,

THE SCIENTIFIC METHOD

Scientists are people who like to learn new things. They watch and look at the world. They ask questions. You are like a scientist. You look and watch to learn. You ask questions, too.

A scientist uses steps when they work. These steps are called the scientific method. Here are the steps. You can use the scientific method just like a scientist.

1. **Problem**   What do I want to know?

2. **Hypothesis**   What do I think will happen?

3. **Experimentation** What will I need? What will I do?

4. **Observation**   What happened?

5. **Conclusion**   Why did it happen?

6. **Comparison**   Was I right in Step 2? If I was not right, what did I learn?

7. **Presentation**   How can I show the class about my work?

8. **Resources**   What books did I use? Who wrote these books? Who helped me do the work at home?

Name _____   Date _____

THE SCIENCE FAIR

The world is a fun place. There are many things to learn. You can learn by watching. You can learn by reading. You can even test things to learn about them.

At a science fair, you can show what you learned. It takes hard work to do a good job. You must plan. How long will it take to read about your idea? Will you need to build something? What will you do to show off your work?

Here is a plan to help you. Think about how much time you need. Fill in the chart to keep you on track.

The name of my work is _____.
Here is my plan.

		Start Date	End Date
1.	Choose something to learn about		
2.	Look in books or talk to people		
3.	Write down facts		
4.	Write a hypothesis		
5.	Get things to do the work		
6.	Test or make a model		
7.	Think about what you did or made		
8.	Write a story telling what you did — make it neat		
9.	Plan how to show your work with pictures and charts		
10.	Set up your work		
11.	Finish writing any facts		
12.	Think about what you learned		

Good luck!

Life Science 2, SV 3842-5

Name _____ Date _____

UNIT 1 ASSESSMENT: THE LIVING WORLD

Directions: Circle the letter of the correct word to complete each sentence.

1. The natural home of a plant or an animal is called a _____.
   a. forest   **b.** habitat   **c.** shelter

2. An _____ is everything around a living thing.
   a. environment   **b.** animal   **c.** ocean

3. Plants and animals _____ with each other in their environments.
   a. play   **b.** learn   **c.** interact

4. Name a hot, dry habitat. _____

5. Name a warm, wet habitat. _____

6. Tell four things that living things need.

   a. _____

   b. _____

   c. _____

   d. _____

7. Why do all living things need plants? _____

   _____

8. What does pollution do to habitats? _____

   _____

© Steck-Vaughn Company   **Unit One: Assessment**
Life Science 2, SV 3842-5

Name _____ Date _____

Unit 2 Assessment: Plants

A. Directions: Use the words from the box to fill in the blanks.

1. The _____ of a plant hold it in the ground.

2. _____ moves from the roots to the leaves through the _____ .

3. The _____ make food for the plant.

4. The plant uses air, water, and _____ to make _____ .

5. _____ are plants that cannot make their own food.

6. _____ grow into new plants.

7. _____ stems are strong and hard.

8. Pine tree leaves are called _____ .

9. Roots get water from the _____ .

food
roots
stem
Seeds
Water
leaves
Tree
sunlight
soil
needles
fungi

B. Directions: Draw a picture of a flower. Label its <u>roots</u>, <u>stem</u>, and <u>leaves</u>.

- Write **a** on the part of the plant that makes food.
- Write **b** on the part of the plant that carries food and water through the plant.
- Write **c** on the part of the plant that carries water from the soil to the plant.
- Write **d** on the part of the plant that makes seeds.

Name _____   Date _____

UNIT 3 ASSESSMENT: ANIMALS

A. Directions: Complete the chart about animals.
Some spaces are filled in for you.

Kind of Animal	How It Looks or Feels	How It Moves (most often)	How It Gives Birth	Name an Animal
	has fur, soft			hamster
Reptile		slithers		
Amphibian			eggs in water	
	has scales			
Bird			eggs in nest	
		crawls		ant

B. Directions: Under the name of each place, draw an animal
that lives there. Write what the animal is.

Desert	Forest	Ocean

C. Directions: Answer the questions.

1. How do scientists find out about animals that lived years ago?

_____

2. Give one reason why an animal might become endangered.

_____

Unit Three: Assessment
Life Science 2, SV 3842-5

UNIT 4 ASSESSMENT: HEALTH AND SAFETY

A. Use these words to fill in the blanks.

teeth	foods	burning	bicycle	safe
energy	rest	inside	street	alone

1. Your body uses _____ to run, jump, and swim.

2. Healthy _____ give you energy.

3. It is important to get plenty of _____.

4. It is not _____ to play in the street.

5. Never swim _____.

6. Brush your _____ after eating.

7. Use correct hand signals when riding your _____.

8. Get out of a _____ building quickly.

9. Get _____ during a thunderstorm.

10. Look both ways before you cross the _____.

B. Choose a sense you can use to learn about each thing. Write the letter of each thing by the sense.

11. sight _____   a. rose

12. smell _____   b. bunny

13. touch _____   c. ice cream

14. hearing _____   d. smoke

15. taste _____   e. radio

Unit 1: The Living World
Background Information

Living/Nonliving

All living things carry on activities that nonliving things do not. These life processes define a living thing. All living things grow, or increase in size and in the amount of matter they contain. All living things can reproduce, or make more of the same kind of organism. Living things consume energy, change it, and excrete, or give off, waste. Living things react to stimuli and to changes in the environment.

Nonliving things may carry on some of these activities, but because they do not carry on all of these activities, they are not living. Students may be confused about what is living and what is not. Water seems to move, change, and appear alive. A flame will flicker and grow. Even scientists disagree about certain things, such as viruses. Distinguishing between living and nonliving things can be difficult, but students can follow the guidelines above to form a strong grasp of the concept.

The Web of Life: Life Cycles, Communities, and Food Chains

All living things go through life cycles. From single-celled organisms to the largest animals, these life cycles include growth, change, consumption of food and water, use of energy, reproduction, and death. Reproduction varies among life forms. Plants reproduce by seeds or spores. Animals may lay eggs or give birth to live young. Some offspring resemble the parents and others do not. Some animals, such as frogs, undergo metamorphosis, or a complete change, during their lifetimes. The successful reproduction of a species is important to that population's continued growth or stability.

Populations are plants or animals of one kind that live in one area. Scientists are interested in keeping track of population numbers so that they can tell if a population is in danger of extinction. The life cycles of animals are studied to see how and why populations increase and decrease.

A typical food chain begins with plants. Most plants make their own food. Algae make their food from nonliving things. Plant cells have chloroplasts, which trap energy from the Sun. Water and carbon dioxide enter the cell through the cell wall. The cell turns the water and gas into food and oxygen. The cell uses the food and passes off the oxygen to be used by other living things. Plants also produce sugar and starch, which are used by other animals. The animals that use plants are herbivores (plant eaters), carnivores (meat eaters who eat the plant eaters), and omnivores (plant and animal eaters). The animals give off carbon dioxide, which is used by the plants. Food webs are used to describe overlapping food chains. These communities and the interactions within them are complex. When their natural order is disrupted, the balance of nature is affected, and organisms can be in danger. The most dire consequence of this disruption is the extinction of a species.

The relationships between organisms in a community can be described in three ways. If the relationship between two organisms is beneficial to both, it is called mutualism. If the relationship helps one organism while the other is neither helped nor harmed, it is called commensalism. If the relationship helps one organism and harms the other, it is known as parasitism.

A community contains food makers, or producers, food takers, or consumers, and decomposers. Typically, the producers are plants. Both other plants and animals eat plants. Carnivores also need plants, as they live off the animals that eat plants. Consumers eat plants, animals, or plants and animals. An animal that eats another animal is a predator. The animal that is eaten is the prey. When the producers and consumers die, they begin to change—they rot and decay. The decomposers get their food from wastes and dead organisms. Molds, yeast, and bacteria break down the dead matter and give off carbon dioxide. The carbon dioxide is then used by green plants to make food.

Adaptations to Environment

In order for living things to remain alive, they must respond to changes or conditions in the environment. Environments include all the conditions in which a living thing exists. This includes the food the organism needs, water, soil, air, temperature, and climate. Common environments are deserts, grasslands, oceans, and forests. Each of these larger environments contains many smaller environments. There are ponds and swamps in the forest. Deserts can be hot or cold. The living and nonliving things in each environment interact with each other to survive. When environments are threatened or changed in drastic ways, the living things in the environment are also threatened.

Animals and plants are adapted to their environments. Adaptations occur through structures and behaviors. The structures include the physical makeup of plants and animals. Behaviors, which are easier to observe in animals, include things like migration and hibernation. In winter, many birds migrate to warmer climates in the South. Some animals, like moose and caribou, also have migratory routes. Many animals hibernate, or sleep, through the winter months. They work through the fall to store food in their bodies that carries them through the winter months. While they sleep, their body processes slow.

The Human Factor

Organisms need to adapt to and change with the changes in their environment to survive. If they cannot adapt, they will not survive. Organisms adapt through physical changes that help them live in their particular habitats and through habits, such as migration, that help them survive. Although many events can disrupt a community and its balance, humans have had the greatest impact upon the Earth's environment. Humans need not only food and energy but also power and space for settlement. Humans create wastes that are not natural to the environment. This environmental pollution is an important concern for everyone. If it is not controlled, the balance of nature is disrupted, organisms die, and those that depend upon the dead organisms may die. It is crucial for humans to find ways to live without creating such disturbances in the environment.

HOMES ARE HABITATS

A **habitat** is the natural home of a plant or animal. It is the place where a plant or an animal lives and grows on its own. Oceans, deserts, forests, and rain forests are habitats. Many plants and animals live in each of these habitats.

Draw a line from each animal to its habitat.

1.

2.

3.

4.

Unit 1: The Living World

Life Science 2, SV 3842-5

ANIMALS AND THEIR NEEDS

A garden is a habitat. A habitat is a place where an animal or a plant lives. It has all the things in it that the living thing needs: food, water, air, and shelter.

In the garden, animals find leaves or other food they need to eat. When it rains, the water is trapped in the soil or on leaves. This is used by the animals. They can get the air they need above ground or below ground. The animals find shelter under rocks, leaves, or underground.

What are the four things an animal needs in its habitat?

1. _____

2. _____

3. _____

4. _____

ANIMALS IN THE GARDEN

Many animals live in garden habitats. Some live above the ground. Some live below the ground. The plants help the animals in the garden. Some of the animals help the plants, too. Both the animals and the plants find what they need to live in the garden.

Color the animals that live above the ground. Circle the animals that live below the ground.

EARTHWORMS

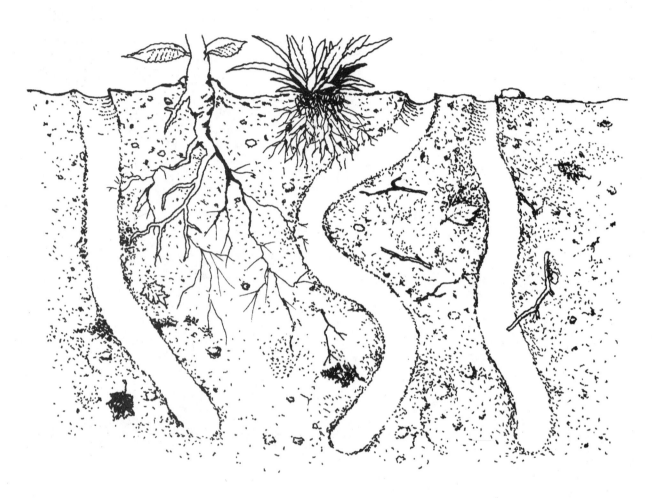

Worms are animals that live in gardens. Worms tunnel through the ground. The tunnels help air and water get into the soil. They give roots room to grow. Worms leave droppings that are good for plants.

Plants help worms, too. Worms eat dead parts of plants as they tunnel through the soil.

Draw worms in these underground tunnels.
Show what they are eating.

WET OR DRY?

This is a **desert**. The hot Sun heats up the dry sand and rocks. There is little or no water around because it doesn't rain much in a desert. Few plants can grow there.

desert

This is a **rain forest**. It rains almost every day in a rain forest. Water drips from the leaves of plants. It flows in rivers and streams. Many plants grow in this habitat.

rain forest

Circle the word that tells about each habitat.

1. desert   dry   wet

2. rain forest   dry   wet

DESERT HIDE-AND-SEEK

Some animals live in deserts. They often hide from the hot Sun. Small ones crawl under rocks. Some go into holes in the ground. Coyotes and other large animals hide in caves. They rest during the day. Then at night they hunt for food. They get some of the water they need from the plants and animals they eat.

What is wrong with the picture below? Mark an X on each animal that does <u>not</u> live in a desert.

20

THIS PLACE IS DRY!

There is little water for plants in the desert. Desert plants store water in their stems. Then they can get the water they need, even when it doesn't rain for a long time.

The **cactus** plant grows in the desert. It has a thick skin that protects it from the hot weather. It also has sharp needles that keep some animals from eating it.

Find the cacti in the picture. Then color their stems green and their needles brown.

Name _____ Date _____

MAKE A DESERT HOME

You can make a desert home.

> **Materials:**
> • a large jar • desert plants • sandy soil • rocks
> • a spoon • garden gloves

Do This

A. Put some sandy soil and rocks in the jar.

B. Put some desert plants in the jar.
Be sure to wear gloves.

C. Place the jar in a sunny place.

D. Water the plants every two or three weeks.

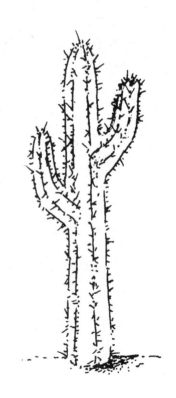

HERE OR THERE

A monkey likes to eat soft fruits like bananas. A desert does not have these fruits. That is why the monkey does not live in a desert. It lives in a rain forest. There it can find the foods it likes to eat. And it can find plenty of water to drink, too.

Rain forest animals usually cannot live in a desert. Desert animals usually cannot live in a rain forest. Each plant or animal lives in a habitat that meets its own needs.

Circle each plant or animal that grows in a hot, wet habitat.

1.

2.

3.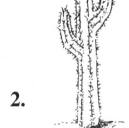

4.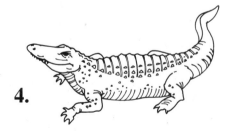

5.

6.

Name _____ Date _____

THIS PLACE IS WET!

This is Jane's plant. One day after she planted it, she saw drops of water on the side of the jar. "Where did this water come from?" Jane asked.

"This is what happens," said Jane's teacher. "The plants take up water from the soil. The plants give off some water into the air. Water also moves from the soil into the air. The lid on the jar keeps the air inside. Then the Sun warms the air in the jar. And the water comes back out of the air in little drops. So the plants can use the same water over and over again."

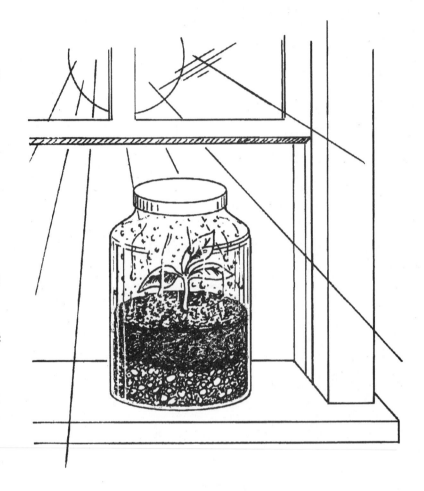

Where did the water on the side of the jar come from? Circle two things in the picture to show your answer.

24

ALL TOGETHER NOW!

The garden habitat is an environment. An **environment** is everything around a living thing. There are plants, animals, rocks, water, soil, and air in a garden environment.

Plants and animals interact with each other in their environments. **Interact** means to affect each other in different ways. For example, plants can be food for animals. Animals can carry the seeds of plants to other places.

Draw a picture of your environment.
Show the living and nonliving things.

A SALTY WORLD

The water in oceans is salty. This water is called **salt water**. But water in lakes, ponds, rivers, and streams is not salty. It is called **fresh water**.

A change of habitat can harm a plant or animal. Sea plants and animals need the salt water of an ocean to live. They could not live in the fresh water of a lake or pond. And the plants and animals in a lake or pond could not live in the salty ocean.

Draw a picture of a water animal that could <u>not</u> live in fresh water.

Underwater Life

Sharks and stingrays swim through ocean waters. Lobsters and crabs creep about on ocean floors.

Some sea animals eat plants for food. Some eat other animals. Sea animals get their food in different ways. Sharks use their sharp teeth. Jellyfish and octopuses use their tentacles. Crabs and lobsters use their claws. Stingrays and sea anemones use their stingers.

1. Find the sea animals that are numbered 1 to 7.

2. Mark an X on the part that each animal uses to catch its food.

OCEAN FOOD CHAIN

Number the pictures to show the order of a food chain.
Then answer the questions.

1. What would happen to the small fish if the plants were gone?

   _____

   _____

2. What would happen to the big fish if the small fish were gone?

   _____

   _____

3. If the plants were gone, would the people catch any fish?

   _____

   _____

4. Why do all living things need plants?

   _____

   _____

   _____

CIRCLE OF LIFE

Living things can become endangered or extinct because their habitat is changed or destroyed. A **habitat** is a place where an animal or plant lives. A habitat has all the things in it that the living thing needs: food, water, air, and shelter. Habitats are changed when trees are cut down, grassland is plowed under, and swamps are drained. Air pollution, acid rain, and the use of poisons also change or destroy habitats.

1. **Color this forest habitat.**
2. **On another piece of paper, tell why these animals and plants live in this habitat.**

29

Name _____ Date _____

TROUBLE IN THE GREAT OUTDOORS

Pollution is something that spoils a habitat. A soft-drink can tossed out a car window is pollution. A tire in a stream is pollution. Empty bags, plastic cups, and bottle caps are pollution, too. Even fishing line is pollution. So is a used paper diaper.

People cause pollution problems. People can solve pollution problems, too. They help by cleaning up their own trash wherever they are. They also help by cleaning up other people's trash at roadsides, parks, and beaches.

Circle the pollution people can clean up in the park.

SECOND LIFE

Pollution is everywhere. It is in lakes, rivers, streams, and oceans. It is in forests. It is in deserts. And more and more, it is in rain forests. Pollution harms the land, water, and air in habitats around the world.

Many people recycle some of their trash to help solve pollution problems. They sort the trash into bins so it can be used again.

1. Draw an empty can in the correct bin.
2. Draw an old newspaper in the correct bin.

OVER AND OVER—MAKING PAPER

The workers in a paper mill grind up trees to make wood pulp. Then they process the wood pulp into sheets of paper.

Old newspapers and brown bags are recycled. They are used to make more pulp. So, trash is used over and over again to make paper. You can make paper, too.

Read the steps below. Write the letter of the missing word in each blank.

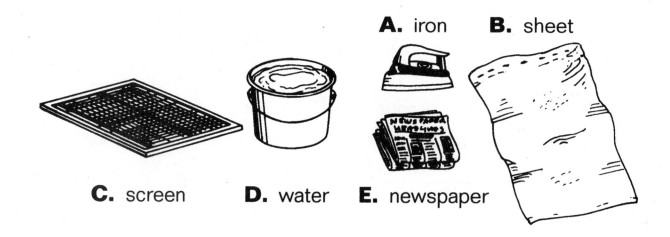

A. iron **B.** sheet **C.** screen **D.** water **E.** newspaper

How You Can Make Paper

1. Tear old _____ into small pieces.

2. Soak the pieces in _____ until you have paste.

3. Spread the pulp on a _____, and let it dry.

4. Remove the pulp, place a _____ on it, and

   _____ it.

5. Peel the paper off the _____.

UNIT 1 SCIENCE FAIR IDEAS

A science fair project can help you to understand the world around you better. Choose a topic that interests you. Then use the scientific method to develop your project. Here is an example:

1. **PROBLEM:** Is mold a living thing?
2. **HYPOTHESIS:** Mold has the characteristics of a living thing.
3. **EXPERIMENTATION:** Observe mold. Place a piece of bread and a piece of fruit in a plastic bag. Add two or three drops of water. Put the bag in a dark place for a few days. Observe the bag each day. Record what you see.
4. **OBSERVATION:** The fruit and the bread became moldy. Mold grew on the food. The mold used the food for energy. The mold grew. The mold made more mold, or reproduced.
5. **CONCLUSION:** Mold has the characteristics of a living thing.
6. **COMPARISON:** Conclusion agrees with hypothesis.
7. **PRESENTATION:** Show your experiment. Set up three test bags at different stages. (Start one bag 4 days before the fair, start one 3 days before, and one 2 days before.) Show what you wrote when you observed the bags each day.
8. **RESOURCES:** Tell of any reading you did to help you with your experiment. Tell who helped you to get materials or set up your experiment.

Other Project Ideas

1. How do living things help or harm each other?
2. Can living things survive in different environments?
3. Can you create a habitat for living things?
4. How can nonliving things help living things?

Unit 2: Plants
Background Information

Classification

The plant kingdom contains about 450,000 different kinds of plants, which are each classified into several divisions. The four main classifications for plants are:

- algae (almost all live in water; from microscopic single-celled plants to seaweed);
- bryophyta (mosses and liverworts; live in moist places; produce spores);
- pteridophyta (ferns, clubmosses, horsetails; no flowers); and
- spermatophyta (largest group—over 350,000 species; reproduce by way of seeds).

Spermatophytes are divided into two categories, the gymnosperms and the angiosperms. Gymnosperms, or "naked seed" plants, have seeds in cones, like pinecones from conifer trees. The angiosperms, or "covered seed" plants, include all of the flowering plants.

Flowering plants are the most numerous type of plant on Earth. They are further classified into groups. Some of the common groups of flowering plants are:

- grass family (corn, sugar, barley, rice, wheat);
- lily family (violets, hyacinths, tulips, onions, asparagus);
- palm family (coconut, date);
- rose family (strawberries, peaches, cherries, apples, and other fruits);
- legume family (peas, beans, peanuts);
- beech family; and
- composite family (sunflowers and others with flowers that are actually many small flowers).

Fungi are sometimes classified with plants, and sometimes they are not. A two-kingdom classification includes molds and fungi with plants, while a three-kingdom system does not. This is because molds and fungi lack chlorophyll and cannot produce their own food. They also lack roots, stems, and leaves, and they reproduce from spores that are distributed through the air or water.

Plants are also classified as vascular and nonvascular. Vascular plants have tubes that bring the liquids the plants need from their environment up through the plants. The tubes also help to support the plants. Nonvascular plants, such as mosses, do not have tubes. They are shorter because they must remain close to their source of moisture. They get the water and nutrients they need through their root systems.

Photosynthesis

Most plants are green. Green plants are green because they contain chlorophyll, most of which is in the leaves. There are some plants that contain chlorophyll but whose leaves are not green. This is because the chlorophyll has been masked by other pigmentation in the plant. Chlorophyll is necessary for the making of food, but the chlorophyll itself is not used in the food that is made.

Photosynthesis depends on light. A plant that is deprived of light loses its chlorophyll (and its ability to make food) and eventually will die. Plants take in energy from the Sun and carbon, oxygen, and hydrogen from the air and water. They change these raw materials into carbohydrates and oxygen. The carbohydrates are used and stored in the plants for food. The oxygen is released into the air and water where the plants live. In this way, plants constantly replenish the Earth's oxygen supply.

Mushrooms and molds are not green because they do not have chlorophyll. They cannot make their own food. Molds and mushrooms depend on other organisms for their food. Mushrooms and molds are fungi.

Reproduction

Plants reproduce from seeds in flowers, from seeds in cones, or from spores. The seeds form after fertilization of their egg cells by male cells from pollen grains. Pollen can be carried to the egg cells by bees or other insects, by the wind, or by animals.

Seeds contain tiny plants called embryos around which a store of food is packed. In some seeds, such as bean seeds, the food is stored inside the embryo. Seeds are spread by animals and the wind. When the seeds in a cone are ripe, the cone opens and the seeds float to the ground or are carried by the wind. Some seeds have tiny parachutes to help them drift. A seed needs moisture, warmth, and oxygen to begin growing into a new plant. If conditions are not right for germination, some seeds can remain in a resting state for hundreds of years.

Ocean Plants

Ocean plants differ from land plants in several ways. Ocean plants grow in salt water. They are often very small and must be viewed through a microscope. The ones that we can see are many different colors, whereas the plants on land are mostly green. Most ocean plants need sunlight to live, and they grow in shallow

water. Ocean plants often do not have roots, stems, or leaves. Some are anchored to rocks, and some have air bladders that allow them to float near the surface of the ocean. People have found many uses for the ocean plant kelp, a type of seaweed. It is a source of food for many people. It is also used to make fertilizer, medicines, and ice cream.

Life Cycle

The life cycle of a seed plant begins with an embryo. An embryo is an undeveloped living thing that comes from a fertilized egg. The eggs in a flowering plant are called ovules. When the ovules are fertilized, they begin to grow. A seed is a complete embryo plant surrounded by the food it needs to grow and protected by a coating. When the seed is planted, or lands on the ground, it begins to sprout. It grows into a seedling and then an adult plant that develops flowers in which new seeds grow.

PLANTS IN THE GARDEN

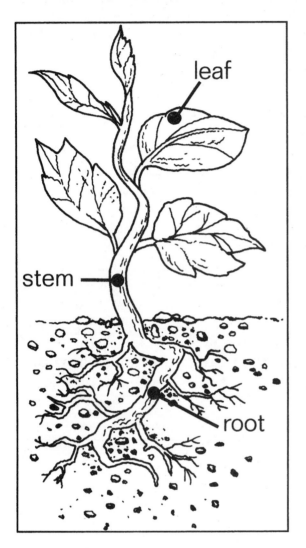

   Plants are one of the things in a garden. Like other living things, plants need food, water, and air to live. Most plants have three parts: **roots**, **stems**, and **leaves**. These plant parts use the food, water, and air in different ways to keep the whole plant alive.

Draw a plant that you have seen. Draw and label the roots, stems, and leaves.

ROOTS

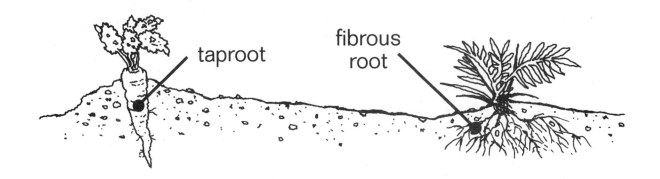

taproot

fibrous root

Roots help a plant by holding it in the ground. Roots also take in water and **nutrients** from the **soil**. Nutrients help make plants healthy.

There are two kinds of roots. A **taproot** is long and thick. It can get water and nutrients that are deep in the soil. A carrot is a taproot. The other kind of root is a **fibrous root**. These roots are short and thin. They get water and nutrients that are near the top of the soil. Grass has fibrous roots.

Finish this chart. Use the words in the box.

short long thick thin	taproot	fibrous roots

Life Science 2, SV 3842-5

How Does Water Get Into a Plant?

Materials:
- glass • toothpicks • red food coloring • potato • knife • water

Do This

A. Put toothpicks into the sides of a potato.

B. Put some water in a glass. Mix red food coloring with the water.

C. Put the potato into this mixture.

D. Wait a few days. Cut the potato in half.

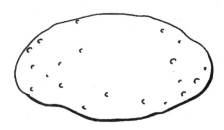

What do you see?

1. How did the potato change?

_____

_____

_____

What do you think?

2. Tell why the potato changed.

_____

_____

_____

STEMS

Stems are very important parts of plants. Stems carry the water and nutrients from the roots of plants to their leaves. Stems carry food to all parts of plants. Stems also hold plants up toward the Sun's light. Without light, plants would die.

Draw ↑ to show how water travels through this plant.

Name _____ Date _____

How Does Water Travel Through a Plant?

Materials:
- glass jar • red food coloring • stalk of celery with leaves
- magnifying glass • water • table knife

Do This

A. Mix food coloring in some water.

B. Put a stalk of celery into the water.

C. Wait a day. Look at the leaves.

D. Cut off a piece of the stalk.

What do you see?

1. What happened to the leaves?

_____

_____

2. What did you see when you cut the stalk?

_____

_____

What do you think?

3. Tell how water travels to the leaves of a plant.

_____

_____

ROOTS AND STEMS

1. We eat some roots and stems uncooked.
   Carrots and radishes are roots.
   Scallions and celery are stems.

2. Clean some of these vegetables.
   Cut them up.

3. Cut radishes like this.
   Put them in cold water.
   They will open up and look like flowers.

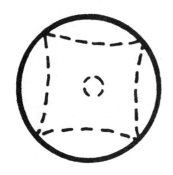

4. Put the vegetables on a plate.
   You can make a design with them.

5. Serve these healthy foods with lunch or dinner.

Name _____ Date _____

LEAVES

Leaves grow in many shapes and sizes. Each kind of plant has its own kind of leaves. But leaves can be sorted into three main kinds.

This is a broad leaf. It is wide. Maple and oak trees have broad leaves.

These are narrow leaves. Just as their name says, they are narrow! Grasses have narrow leaves.

These are needle leaves. They are narrow and pointed, like a needle. Fir and pine trees have needle leaves.

On another sheet of paper, draw some leaves. Write whether they are broad, narrow, or needle leaves.

LEAVES AT WORK

Leaves help a plant by making food for it. The leaves use sunlight, water, and air to make the food. Then the stem carries this food back through the rest of the plant. Without food, the plant could not grow flowers and seeds.

Draw two things that are needed for this plant to make food for itself.

Name _____   Date _____

DOES A LEAF GIVE OFF WATER?

Materials:
- cardboard • potted plant • large glass jar • petroleum jelly

---

Do This

A. Put a plant on a piece of cardboard.

B. Put clear jelly around the rim of a large glass jar.

C. Put the jar over the plant.
What do you think will happen?

_____

_____

D. Wait a few days.

What do you see?

1. What happened to the inside of the jar?

_____

_____

What do you think?

2. Tell why this happened.

_____

_____

© Steck-Vaughn Company

Unit 2: Plants
Life Science 2, SV 3842-5

Name _____ Date _____

SEEDS

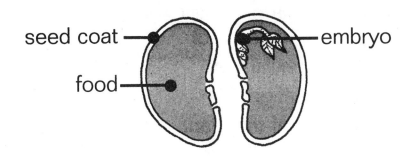

seed coat — ● food — ● — embryo

Seeds are found in the flower of a plant. Seeds are many shapes and sizes. On the outside of a seed is a **seed coat**. The seed coat protects the seed. Inside the seed are the **embryo** and food for the embryo. An embryo is a tiny plant that will grow into a bigger plant.

Draw four seeds of different shapes and sizes.
Write what kind of seed each one is.

1. _____	2. _____
3. _____	4. _____

Unit 2: **Plants**

Life Science 2, SV 3842-5

FROM SEED TO PLANT

Most seeds can sprout without soil. But to grow into plants, seeds need soil, water, air, and warmth. When they get what they need, plants can grow quickly.

In each box, draw one thing a seed needs to grow. Write on the line what it needs.

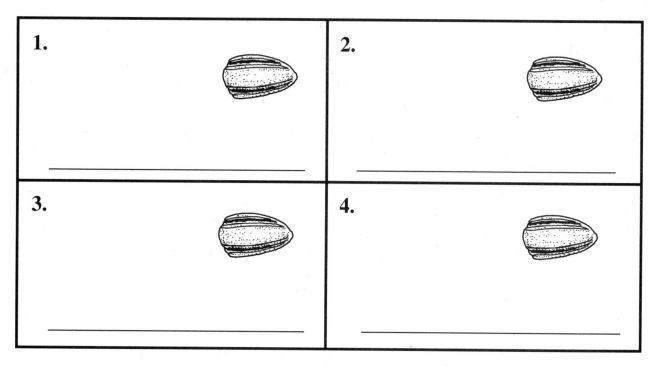

A growing plant can be very strong. A plant can push aside things that are in its way as it grows. A plant can move soil, gravel, and even rocks while it is growing.

Name _____ Date _____

IN WHAT WEATHER DO SEEDS GROW BEST?

Materials:
- 2 dishes • 4 towels • seeds • refrigerator • water

Do This

A. Put a wet towel in each of two dishes.

B. Put some seeds on the towels.

C. Cover the seeds with another wet towel.

D. Put one dish in a warm place. Put the other dish in a cool place, like the refrigerator.

E. Check the seeds every day. Keep the towels moist.

What do you see?

1. Which seeds grew faster?

_____

_____

_____

What do you think?

2. Tell what weather is best for growing seeds.

_____

_____

_____

Name _____ Date _____

HOW ARE SEEDS DIFFERENT?

Materials:
- seeds • paper towels • pencil • paste • 3 x 5 index cards

Do This

A. Collect many kinds of seeds.

B. Dry them on paper towels.

C. Glue each kind of seed to a card.
Write the name of the plant it comes from.

D. Put the seeds in groups.

What do you see?

1. How did you group the seeds?

_____

_____

2. What did you name each group?

_____

_____

What do you think?

3. Tell some of the differences between the seeds.

_____

_____

_____

Name _____ Date _____

SEEDS WE EAT

Circle the foods that are seeds.

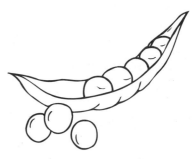

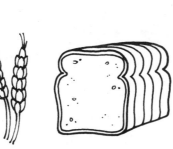

MAKING SPROUTS

Materials:
- alfalfa seeds or mung beans • jar • spoon • water • cheesecloth

Do This

A. Put a large spoonful of seeds in a jar.

B. Cover the seeds with water.

C. Soak the seeds overnight.

D. Put cheesecloth over the jar.

E. Rinse the seeds. Pour off extra water.

F. Put the jar in a dark place.

G. Rinse the seeds three times a day.

In about five days, your sprouts will be ready to eat!

Name _____ Date _____

SOILS FOR PLANTING

Plants that grow well in one kind of soil may not grow well in another. That is why people who plant gardens use special kinds of soil when they plant.

Clay holds a lot of water, but it gets hard. Roots can't grow well in it. The roots of a plant can spread out in sandy soil. But sand doesn't hold water well. Potting soil is clay and sand mixed together.

Would plants grow well in potting soil? Tell why or why not.

What Is in Soil?

There are little holes in the soil underground. The holes are filled with air. The air spaces give a plant's roots room to grow.

There is another reason for the holes underground. When it rains, the holes fill with water. The water mixes with nutrients in the soil. Then the roots of plants take the water and the nutrients from the soil into the plants.

Draw a picture of how you think the soil looks underground.

WHAT KIND OF SOIL IS BEST FOR PLANTS?

Plant some bean seeds three ways.

Materials:
- sand • soil • 3 cups, paper or plastic • bean seeds

Do This

A. Put only sand in one cup. Label it *Cup A.*

B. Put only soil in one cup. Label it *Cup B.*

C. Put sand and soil in one cup.
Label it *Cup C.*

D. Then put seeds in each cup.
Put the cups near a window.
Water them when needed.

E. Which seeds grow best? Keep this record.

	Date seeds came up	Date beans had 2 leaves	Date beans had 3 leaves
SAND Cup A			
SOIL Cup B			
SAND AND SOIL Cup C			

WHAT HAPPENS TO PLANTS IN THE COLD?

Materials:
- 2 small stems from a houseplant
- 2 small stems from an evergreen tree
- 2 plastic or paper cups
- water

Do This

A. Put water in the cups.

B. Put one of each stem in the cups.

C. Put one cup in the freezer.
Leave the other cup in the room.

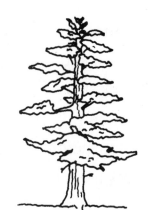

What do you see?

1. Look at the stems the next day.
What happened? _____

_____

What do you think?

2. Could houseplants live outside in freezing weather?

_____

3. Could evergreen trees live outside in freezing weather?

_____

Name _____ Date _____

Do Plants Need Sunlight and Air?

Materials:
- potted plant • black paper • plastic bag • twist tie • paper clip

Do This

A. Cover a leaf on a plant with black paper. It will not get sunlight.

B. Cover another leaf with a plastic bag. This leaf will not get air.

C. Write down what you think will happen to each leaf.

D. Wait a week. Uncover the leaves.

What do you see?

1. How does each leaf look now?

_____

_____

What do you think?

2. Do plants need air? Tell why you think so.

_____

_____

3. Do plants need sunlight? Tell why you think so.

_____

_____

Name _____ Date _____

OCEAN PLANTS

Unscramble the words.
Use them to fill in the blanks.

NTLPAS	ULGSNIHT	RLOCOS
LTAS	IRSMCOOPCE	LOFAT
	LLSHWOA	

1. Ocean _____ are different from land plants.

2. Ocean plants live in _____ water.

3. Some ocean plants _____ in water.

4. Most large ocean plants live in

   _____ water.

5. Some ocean plants are so small that

   you need a _____

   to see them.

6. Plants need _____

   to grow.

7. Ocean plants are many different

   _____.

Name _____ Date _____

How Are Water Plants and Land Plants Different?

Materials:
- grass • geranium • houseplants • eelgrass
- swordplant • seaweed

Do This

A. Look at some land plants and some water plants.

B. Feel them and smell them.

C. Try to stand each one up.

What do you see?

1. Do the water plants and the land plants look the same?

_____

2. Do they feel the same?

_____

3. Do they smell the same?

_____

What do you think?

4. How can you tell if a plant lives in the water or on land?

_____

_____

PLANTS WE EAT

Cut out the pictures below.
Paste them in the correct box.

Seeds	Stems
Flowers	**Roots**

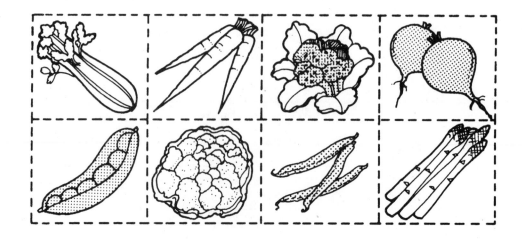

Can Fungi Grow on Food?

Materials:
- bread • apple • clear plastic bag • water • eyedropper • dust

Do This

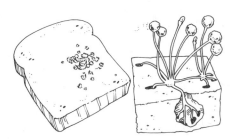

A. Rub some dust on a slice of bread.

B. Put the bread and a slice of apple in a plastic bag.

C. Put ten drops of water in the bag. Close the bag.

D. Put the bag in a warm place. Look at it every day for three days.

What do you see?

1. What changes do you see on the food?

_____

_____

What do you think?

2. Tell if you think it is alive.

_____

_____

_____

3. How do you know?

_____

_____

Name _____ Date _____

GOING THROUGH CHANGES

Trees change as seasons change. Read to find out how a maple tree changes. Then color the pictures to show how a maple tree looks in each season.

spring

The air becomes warmer. Buds open. Little leaves begin to grow on the tree.

summer

The air grows warmer still. Big, green leaves now cover all the branches of the tree.

fall

The air cools off. The leaves on the tree turn yellow and red. They begin to fall.

winter

This is the coldest season. The tree's branches are bare or covered with snowflakes.

Unit 2: Plants
Life Science 2, SV 3842-5

LOOK AT LEAVES

A **forest** is a place where many trees grow. Some trees have broad leaves. Trees with broad leaves are called deciduous trees.

Some trees have needles and cones. They are called evergreens. Evergreens stay green all year. Weather has a lot to do with the kinds of trees that grow in a forest.

broad leaves

needles and cone

1. In the box, draw a forest tree with an animal in it.
2. Circle the kind of tree that you drew.

deciduous   evergreen

TERRIFIC TREES

A tree takes in air through its leaves and gives off water and oxygen through its leaves. The leaves make food for the tree, too. The leaves of an evergreen are its needles.

Draw a line to match the tree to its leaves.

1.

2.

Ferns, wildflowers, and mushrooms grow in forests, too. Each plant grows where it can get the sunlight it needs.

Which things live in a forest? Color them.

3.    **4.**    **5.**

Is It a Plant?

Cut out the sentences at the bottom of the page.
Paste them in the right boxes.

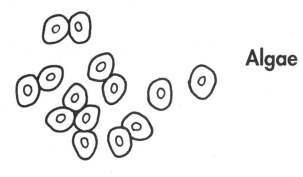

Algae

Fungi

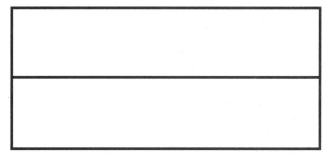

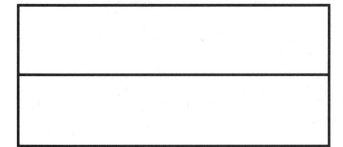

Moss

This is plant-like but has no roots, stems, or flowers.	This living thing can grow on dead plants and animals.
This plant-like living thing lives in water.	This green plant grows in damp, shady places.
This living thing cannot make its own food.	This green plant feels like a soft rug and has no flowers.

PLANT GAME

Name 4 things a plant needs.	Free Space	Name a leaf we eat.	What part of the plant makes seeds?	Where do fruits come from?

Winner

Name 2 ways seeds are spread from place to place.	What part of a plant is the trunk of a tree?	Name a root we eat.	Name 3 things a plant needs to live.	What does the leaf of a plant need to make food?

Free Space	Name a stem we eat.	Free Space	Name 2 things a plant needs.	Name 2 ways people use plants.	There is one kind of root, true or false?	Free Space

What part of the plant makes food for the rest of the plant?	What 2 things do roots do for a plant?	Name 2 things a plants needs to live.	Free Space	Name a fruit we eat.

Name 2 things a stem does for a plant.

Name 1 thing a plant needs to live.	Free Space	Where do roots usually grow?	Name a nut we eat.	Free Space

Start

Name _____   Date _____

Unit 2 Science Fair Ideas

A science fair project can help you to understand the world around you better. Choose a topic that interests you. Then use the scientific method to develop your project. Here is an example:

1. **PROBLEM:** Can plants grow from roots or stems?

2. **HYPOTHESIS:** Plants do not have to grow from seeds.

3. **EXPERIMENTATION:** Get a sweet potato that has eyes. Cut a piece of the potato that has an eye. Put toothpicks in the potato so that you can place it on a glass of water. The eye should be in the water. The toothpicks will keep the potato from sinking in the water. Cut a stem with some leaves from a geranium plant. Place the stem in water but keep the leaves dry. Watch the potato and the geranium cuttings for two weeks. Record what you observe.

4. **OBSERVATION:** Both the potato and the geranium cutting grew roots.

5. **CONCLUSION:** Plants can grow from stems and roots.

6. **COMPARISON:** Conclusion agrees with hypothesis.

7. **PRESENTATION:** Display your experiment. Show the records that you kept. Tell about what you did.

8. **RESOURCES:** Tell of any reading you did to help you with your experiment. Tell who helped you to get materials or set up your experiment.

Other Project Ideas

1. How do seeds move from one place to another?
2. How are fruits and vegetables different?
3. Can a fresh water plant grow in salt water?
4. Why do plants grow well in a greenhouse?

UNIT 3: ANIMALS
BACKGROUND INFORMATION

Classification

The animal kingdom can be classified into two large groups: the vertebrates (those with backbones) and the invertebrates (those without backbones). The backbone supports the body and provides flexibility. The spinal cord extends from the brain through the backbone, or spine. Individual nerves branch out from the spinal cord to different parts of the body. Messages from the brain are sent throughout the body through the spinal cord.

Some animals without backbones are sponges, jellyfish, clams, worms, insects, and spiders. Some of these animals have networks of nerves throughout their bodies with no central nerve cords. Many, like insects, have hard exoskeletons that protect their bodies and give them shape.

Animals are further categorized into six groups:

- Mammals are identified as animals that have hair or fur, feed milk to their young, and are warm-blooded. Warm-blooded animals are able to withstand a wide variety of temperatures and still keep their bodies warm, so they are found almost everywhere. Mammals are vertebrates and breathe through their lungs. Mammals' eggs are fertilized internally, and the babies are born alive. Mammals are capable of learning and have highly developed brains. Some mammals are carnivores (such as lions and dogs) and eat only animals, or meat; some are herbivores (such as rabbits and giraffes) and eat only plants; and some are omnivores (such as bears and skunks) and eat both animals and plants.

- Amphibians are animals that live both on land and in water. They are cold-blooded animals, most with smooth, wet skin. Most lay eggs in the water and move onto the land as they get older. Amphibians undergo a metamorphosis in which their form changes completely. For example, frogs lay their eggs in the water. The eggs grow into tadpoles with heads, gills, and no legs. Then they develop two legs. Later they develop two more legs and lungs, and their tails begin to disappear. Finally, they have four fully grown legs, no tails, and no gills, and they leave the water to live on land. Most amphibians are herbivores when they are born, and carnivores when they become adults living on land. Amphibians can breathe through their skin as well as with their lungs. Most amphibians with legs have webbed feet.

- Reptiles are scaly-skinned, cold-blooded animals. Their body temperatures vary with the temperature of the air around them. Reptiles get energy from the warmth of the Sun. They get sluggish when they are cold. Their skin feels dry and hard. Some reptiles have four legs, and some do not have any legs. Some reptiles bear live young, but most lay eggs. Baby reptiles look much like their parents and can care for themselves from birth. Although many reptiles can swim, they do not breathe under water. They breathe air with their lungs. Reptiles live in forests, jungles, and deserts.

- Birds are the only creatures with feathers. They are warm-blooded vertebrates. Most birds have hollow bones and powerful wing muscles that enable them to fly. Some, such as the ostrich, do not fly. Birds' eggs are fertilized in the body, a protective shell is formed, and the bird lays the egg. Birds care for their young until they are able to fly and get their own food.

- Fish are fitted to their environment because of their gills, which enable them to absorb oxygen from the water. They use their fins and tails to move and are covered with scales. Fish reproduce by external fertilization; the female lays the eggs (spawns) and the male deposits sperm over the eggs. Fish are divided into three groups: jawless fish, cartilage fish, and bony fish. Fish are cold-blooded animals. Their bodies are the temperature of the water in which they live.

- Arthropods are animals without backbones. They have jointed legs, a segmented body, and an exoskeleton. Insects make up the majority of arthropods. Insects have three body parts: the head, the thorax, and the abdomen. The eyes, antennas, and mouths are on the head. Insects have six legs. Some have wings. All insects have a tough exoskeleton. This protects the insect's organs but must be shed as the insect grows. Insects undergo either a complete or an incomplete metamorphosis as they develop from egg to maturity. A complete metamorphosis includes four stages: the egg, the larva, the pupa, and the adult. The incomplete metamorphosis includes an egg stage, a nymph stage, and the adult stage.

Animals Are Suited to Their Environments

Animals live in almost every type of environment on Earth. Each kind of animal has become well suited to its environment through generations of adaptation. Those animals that are not suited to the environment, or that are poorly adapted, do not survive. The animals that are most fit for their environments continue to reproduce and make others like themselves.

Every part of an animal helps it to live in its particular environment. Some animals are colored in ways that help them to blend in with their environments. They are camouflaged to protect them from their enemies. Other animals are brightly colored to attract mates and help them with the continuation of their species. Animals' mouths and teeth are adapted to the types of food that they eat. Meat-eating animals have sharp teeth for tearing and ripping their prey, and other teeth for chewing the meat. Animals that eat leaves and grasses have large flat teeth for chewing.

The beaks and feet of different birds vary greatly. Some birds have thick, short beaks for cracking seeds. Others have long, slender beaks that they dip into flowers to reach nectar. The heron uses its long beak like tweezers to pluck fish from the water. Woodpeckers have beaks strong enough to hammer holes into trees as they look for insects. Eagles have strong, thick claws that enable them to grasp and carry their prey. The webbed feet of ducks help them to swim. Some birds have feet that help them to climb, and others have feet that are best suited for perching.

Insects also have different types of mouth parts depending on their diets; some have chewing mouth parts to eat plants, and others have sucking mouth parts to get liquids.

Most animals are suited to either land or water life. An obvious adaptation for fish is the gills that allow them to breathe in the water. Lungs allow land animals to breathe in air.

Many animals protect themselves with camouflage. Other ways that animals protect themselves are by unique physical defense systems. Skunks emit foul-smelling odors when they are frightened. Porcupines bristle with barbed quills that will embed in the nose of any enemy that gets too close. Other animals have warning systems to alert the rest of a group to danger. Prairie dogs post sentries that will emit a loud whistling sound when danger approaches, and all the prairie dogs will go into their burrows immediately. Many insects have coloring that fools predators. The wings of some moths and butterflies look like large eyes. Predators believe that the insect is larger than it is, and leave it alone. Some animals not only mimic the color of their surroundings, but the shape as well. A walking stick looks just like the sticks and bark among which it makes its home. Yet other animals will change color to fit their changing environments.

Unit 3: Animals
Background Information

Reproduction

All living things have a life cycle within which they take in food and gases, metabolize, excrete waste, reproduce, and die. If living things fail to reproduce or to create healthy offspring, their species will die out. The California condor is one animal whose offspring have failed to thrive. So few condor chicks have survived in recent years that they may be in danger of extinction. It has been found that pesticides concentrated in the bodies of the adult condors have interfered with their reproductive abilities.

Animals reproduce in different ways. Some lay eggs, and others give birth to live young. Some offspring look like their parents, while others do not. Most reptiles, amphibians, fish, and insects lay eggs. The young of many of these animals can move about and find food for themselves soon after they hatch. Birds also lay eggs, but the adult birds remain with the eggs and care for the young until they can find their own food. Most mammals bear live young. The young are fed milk from the mother's body. Mammals spend more time than other animals feeding, protecting, and teaching their young to survive on their own. Animals that give birth to live young have fewer offspring than those that do not tend their young. The young of human beings require more care from their parents than any other animal.

Metamorphosis

The life cycles of some animals include a metamorphosis. A metamorphosis is a complete change in the appearance of an animal. The most striking metamorphosis is the change from caterpillar to butterfly. Metamorphosis is controlled by hormones in the body. When the hormone supply keeping a caterpillar a juvenile stops, the caterpillar begins to become a chrysalis, or pupa. In a frog, the change is controlled by the thyroid gland. Crabs also undergo metamorphosis, and earwigs and grasshoppers undergo incomplete metamorphosis.

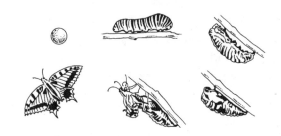

Name _____   Date _____

MAMMALS ARE ANIMALS

Mammals are animals that are covered with hair. Mammals are alike in other ways. A mammal grows inside its mother's body. Then it is born. A young mammal drinks milk from its mother's body.

Most mammals move about on two or four legs. But whales are mammals, even though they don't have legs. Whales have a tiny bit of hair on their smooth skin. A whale is born, and it drinks milk from its mother's body.

Which words tell about a mammal? Write <u>yes</u> or <u>no</u>.

1. has feathers _____

2. has hair on its body _____

3. is born live _____

4. drinks milk from its mother's body _____

Unit 3: Animals
Life Science 2, SV 3842-5

BREAKFAST, LUNCH, AND DINNER

Your teeth have different shapes and sizes. Your front teeth are sharp and pointed. Your back teeth are wide and flat. You use your front teeth to bite and your back teeth to chew.

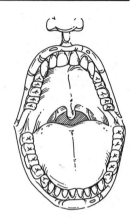

Animals have different teeth, too. Some have sharp teeth for biting foods. Sharp teeth can bite into meat. Others have flat teeth for chewing food. Flat teeth can chew leaves and other parts of plants.

1. Some mammals eat only plants. Draw what their teeth might look like.

2. Some mammals eat only meat. Draw what their teeth might look like.

Name _____ Date _____

STAYING ALIVE!

The elephant is the biggest mammal that lives on land. It can be as tall as a school bus. It can weigh as much as two cars!

Elephants live where the weather is hot. They use their big ears to keep cool. They can flap their ears like fans.

An elephant uses its trunk for many things. It uses its trunk to smell. It can also use the trunk to spray water into its mouth or over its back.

Elephants use their trunks to eat. They can rip up grass. They can also grab leaves and branches off trees. Sometimes they use their trunks to rip up trees!

Color the parts of the elephant you have just read about.

Life Science 2, SV 3842-5

MAMMALS CROSSWORD

Down

1. Mammals have _____ that covers their skin.
3. All mammals are born _____.
4. Mammals drink _____ from their mothers.

Across

2. Mammals are _____ -blooded animals.
5. Mammals breathe with their _____.
6. Mammals take care of their _____.

Name _____   Date _____

WHAT DO MAMMALS EAT?

Materials:
- nature magazines • construction paper • crayons • scissors
- thumbtacks

Do This

A. Find pictures of mammals.

B. Put the pictures into these three groups on a bulletin board.

Mammals That Eat Plants
Mammals That Eat Animals
Mammals That Eat Plants and Animals

What do you see?

1. Which mammals eat plants?

_____

2. Which mammals eat animals?

_____

3. Which mammals eat plants and animals?

_____

What do you think?

4. Do all mammals eat the same things?

_____

Name _____ Date _____

GO FISH!

A. Label the parts of a fish.

a. _____

b. _____

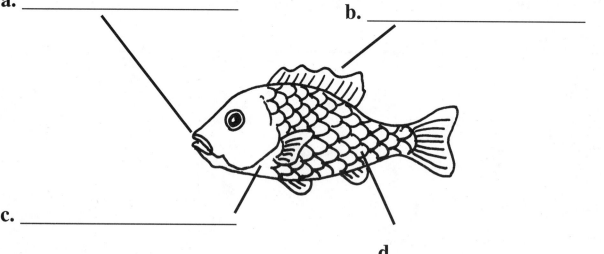

c. _____

d. _____

B. Draw lines to match.

Scales

Gills

Fins

Mouth

• help the fish move.

• helps the fish eat.

• help protect the fish.

• help the fish breathe.

C. List some fish that you know.

1.	4.
2.	5.
3.	6.

Unit 3: Animals
Life Science 2, SV 3842-5

GETTING THE AIR THEY NEED

These are all animals that live in water. Three of these animals are fish. One of them is not a fish. How can you tell?

Like other living things, fish need air. Fish get the air they need from water. Fish have gills. Water flows through the fish's gills. Then, air passes out of the water and into the gills. Blood carries air from the gills to all parts of the fish's body.

Which animal is not a fish? The dolphin. It is a mammal. The dolphin breathes air through its mouth.

Color the fish in the picture.

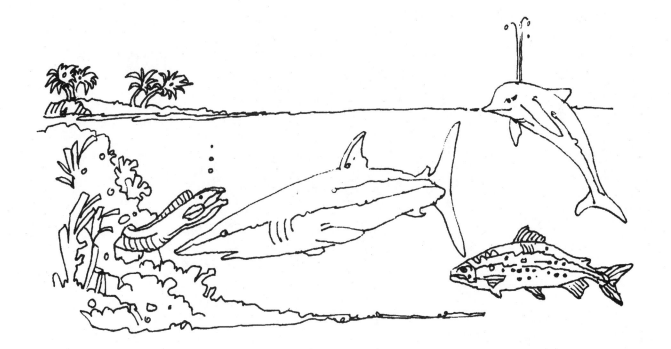

GOING UP!

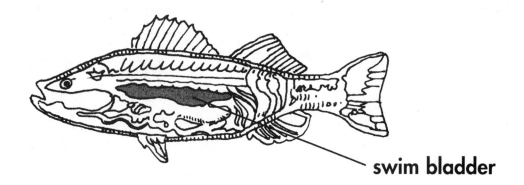

swim bladder

How does this fish move up and down in the water? It has a swim bladder. Air moves in and out of the bladder. When the bladder is full of air, the fish moves up. When the bladder has less air, the fish moves down.

1. Two of these fish have swim bladders that are full of air. Color those fish blue.

2. Two of these fish have swim bladders that have little air. Color those fish yellow.

WHAT HELPS A FISH LIVE IN WATER?

Materials:
- whole fish from a fish market • hand lens or magnifying glass
- paper • pencil

Do This

A. Look at the fish with a hand lens.

B. Draw a picture of what you see.

What do you see?

1. Tell how the scales look.

_____

2. Find the gills. What do they look like? How do they feel?

_____

3. Find the fins. What do they look and feel like?

_____

What do you think?

4. How do scales protect a fish?

_____

5. How do gills help the fish breathe?

_____

6. How do fins help the fish move?

_____

© Steck-Vaughn Company

Unit 3: Animals
Life Science 2, SV 3842-5

Name _____   Date _____

WHAT DO OCEAN ANIMALS LOOK LIKE?

Materials:
- ocean animals • newspaper • magnifying glass • crayons • paper

Do This

A. Look at some ocean animals from a fish market. Touch them.

B. Draw a picture of each one.

What do you see?

1. What do the animals look like?

_____

_____

2. How do they feel?

_____

_____

What do you think?

3. Tell how each animal moves.

_____

_____

4. Tell how they are different from land animals.

_____

_____

Unit 3: Animals
Life Science 2, SV 3842-5

Birds of a Feather

These animals are **birds.** They are alike in several ways. They all have feathers, and they all have wings. Birds hatch from eggs. They also have two legs.

Birds can be many sizes, shapes, and colors. Hummingbirds are some of the smallest birds. One kind of hummingbird is no bigger than your finger. The ostrich is the biggest bird. It can be taller than the tallest person.

Color the pictures of the birds.
Color their feathers to show that birds can look different from one another.

FEED THE BIRDS!

Birds eat many kinds of food. Some birds eat insects. Others eat fish. Some birds eat fruits, while others eat seeds.

Here are some things some children left in a bird feeder for birds to eat. They put them in the feeder in the morning.

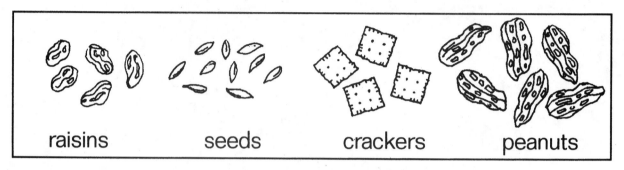

raisins   seeds   crackers   peanuts

Here is what was left in the feeder in the afternoon.

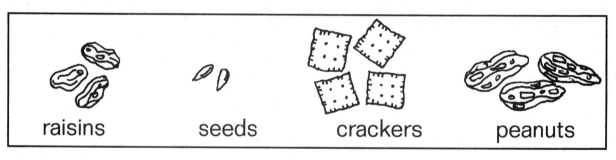

raisins   seeds   crackers   peanuts

1. How many of each food did the birds eat?

   The birds ate _____ raisins, _____ seeds,

   _____ crackers, and _____ peanuts.

2. Which food did the birds like best?

   _____

   _____

WHY ARE A BIRD'S FEATHERS IMPORTANT?

Materials:
- feathers • straw or eyedropper • water

Do This
A. Collect some feathers.
B. Look at the feathers. Feel them.
C. Put a drop of water on each one.

What do you see?
1. Tell what happened to the water on each feather.

_____

_____

What do you think?
2. Do you think birds get wet when it rains? Why?

_____

_____

3. What is another way that feathers are important to a bird?

_____

_____

LOTS OF SCALES

Reptiles are animals that have a body covered with scales. The turtle has scales that fit together like pieces of a puzzle. They look like this.

Snakes have scales that do not fit together like puzzle pieces. Instead, they cover over each other. By themselves, the scales look like this.

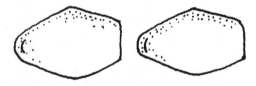

On the snake, the scales look like this.

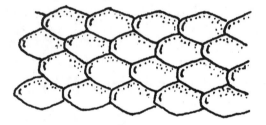

These reptiles are missing their scales. Draw them in.

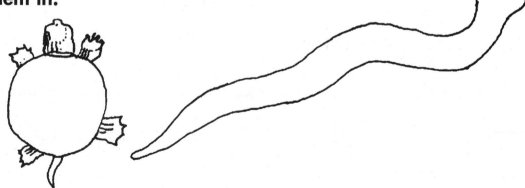

Name _____ Date _____

SNAKING AROUND

Snakes have no legs. How do they move about? Snakes move by crawling. Some snakes crawl forward. Other snakes, like the sidewinder, crawl sideways.

Snakes have fangs, but they have no teeth. How do they eat? Snakes use their fangs to catch their food. Then, they swallow their food whole.

Snakes are covered with scales. What does a snake's skin feel like when you touch it? It feels dry. It does not feel slimy.

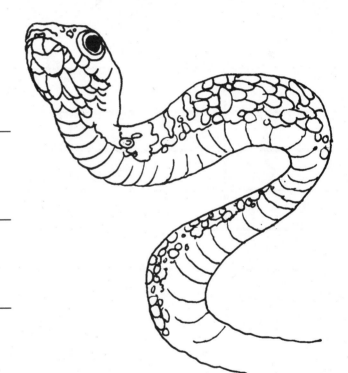

Answer <u>yes</u> or <u>no</u>.

1. Do snakes chew their food?

_____

2. Do all snakes crawl forward?

_____

3. Is a snake's skin slimy?

_____

Name _____ Date _____

How Can You Group Reptiles?

Materials
• nature magazines • animal picture books

Do This

A. Look at reptiles in an animal book.

B. Make a list of all the reptiles you find.

C. Put the reptiles into groups in the chart. What are the names of your groups?

Reptile	Group		

What do you see?

1. How are reptiles in each group the same?

_____

_____

What do you think?

2. Tell another way to group reptiles.

_____

_____

DINOSAUR DAYS

Dinosaurs were reptiles that lived on the Earth millions of years ago. They looked and acted different from each other, just as animals do now. Some dinosaurs were large, and some were small. Some dinosaurs ate plants, and some ate meat. Some walked on two legs, and some walked on four legs.

Paleontologists know about dinosaurs from their observations of fossils and from what they know about living animals. While paleontologists have never seen a living dinosaur, what they know about dinosaurs is based on facts.

Draw a picture of two dinosaurs. Show how dinosaurs can be different from each other.

Name _____   Date _____

SKIN TIGHT

You have probably seen colored pictures of dinosaurs. Most artists paint them brown, gray, or green. But no one really knows what color dinosaurs were. We do know the texture of their skin, because fossils of dinosaur skin have been found.

Dinosaur skin helped dinosaurs live in their environments. Some dinosaur skin may have been brightly colored to look scary to an enemy or to attract other dinosaurs.

Color these dinosaurs to show the way you think they may have looked.

Name _____   Date _____

CONSTRUCT-O-SAURUS

All animals have features that help them live in their habitats. These are called adaptations.

Plant-eating dinosaurs had heavy skin, and many had spikes, horns, or armor. This protected the dinosaurs. Most plant-eating dinosaurs walked on four heavy legs. This would help balance them as they ate.

Meat-eating dinosaurs had lightweight skin to keep them cool during hunting. Many of them moved on two legs and could run quickly when they were chasing prey.

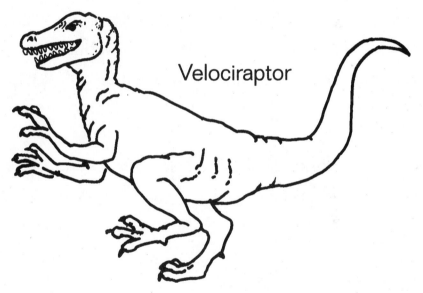

Velociraptor

How did this dinosaur's adaptations help it live in its habitat?

_____

_____

_____

AMAZING AMPHIBIANS

Amphibians are animals that are born in the water and grow to live on the land. They have smooth, wet skin. Amphibians are cold-blooded animals. They use the Sun for energy. Amphibian babies grow from eggs, which are laid in water. As they grow, they undergo a great change. This is called metamorphosis. They grow from eggs to tadpoles with gills and tails. They can breathe in the water. Then they grow legs and lungs. When their tails and gills disappear, they leave the water to live on land.

Most amphibians have legs and webbed feet. When amphibians are young, they eat only plants. When they are older, most amphibians become meat-eaters. Frogs, toads, and salamanders are all amphibians.

Circle the letter of the best answer to complete each sentence.

1. Amphibians have _____ skin.

    a. smooth   **b.** scaly   **c.** dry

2. Amphibians live _____.

    a. on land   **b.** in water   **c.** on land and in water

3. Adult amphibians eat _____.

    a. plants   **b.** meat   **c.** plants and meat

4. What are four stages of an amphibian as it grows? Write your answer.

_____

_____

CAN YOU SHOW A FROG'S LIFE CYCLE?

Materials
- amphibian guidebooks • index cards • string • wire hanger
- hole punch

Do This

A. Look at books about frogs.

B. On different cards, draw each stage of a frog's life:
- egg
- young tadpole with tail
- tadpole with legs
- adult frog

C. Punch holes in the top and bottom of each card.

Use the string to hang them from the hanger in their correct order.

What do you see?

1. In what order did you put your pictures?

_____

_____

What do you think?

2. What other amphibian life cycles could you draw?

_____

_____

Name _____ Date _____

Every Insect!

These animals are **insects.** They are alike in several ways. They all have six legs. They all have three body parts. They have two feelers. Insects have no bones inside their bodies. Instead, they have a skeleton on the outside of their bodies.

1. How many body parts does an insect have?

_____

2. How many legs does an insect have?

_____

3. How many feelers does an insect have?

_____

© Steck-Vaughn Company

Unit 3: Animals
Life Science 2, SV 3842-5

INSIDE OUT

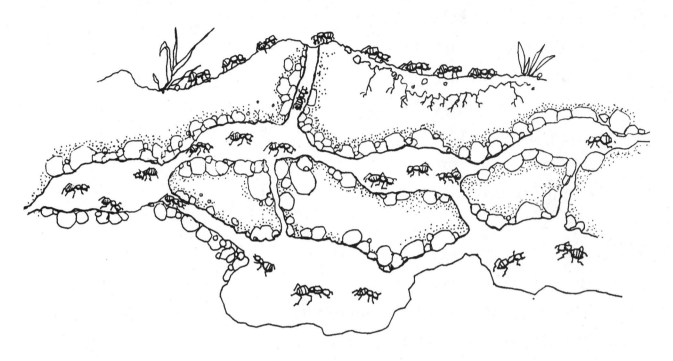

    Some insects, like ants, live and work in large groups. The group is called a colony. They might build nests underground. The nests have many rooms and tunnels.

1. How many rooms are in this colony?

_____

2. How many ants are in this colony?

_____

INSECTS ARE EVERYWHERE

There are more insects than all other animals put together!

Why do you think this is true?

Insects can multiply quickly.

One insect can lay hundreds of eggs.

Insects eat many different things.

Sometimes they cause problems.

Farmers must protect their crops against insects.

Take a walk near your home.

Look for signs of insects.

Can you find leaves that were eaten or chewed?

Can you find fruit that has holes?

Look under old bark and under rocks.

Make a list of everything you find.

HOW DOES AN INSECT MOVE AND EAT?

Materials:
- glass jar • nylon stocking • insect • plant leaves

Do This

A. Look for insects on plants.

B. Put an insect in a jar with some green leaves from the plant.

C. Cover the jar with the stocking.

D. Water the insect. Draw it.

What do you see?

1. How many legs does it have? _____

2. How does the insect move?

_____

_____

3. How does it eat?

_____

_____

What do you think?

4. How can you tell if an animal is an insect?

_____

_____

_____

ANIMAL CHART

Fill in the chart about each animal.
Use books to help you.

Animal	What animal group does it belong to?	Where does the animal live?	Is the animal warm-blooded?	How is it born?	What is its skin covering like?

DIGGING IN

Scientists who are interested in knowing about plants and animals that lived long ago are called **paleontologists.** One way paleontologists find out about the past is by finding and observing fossils.

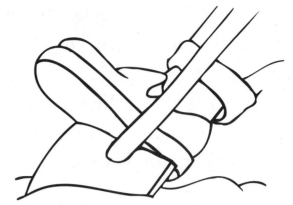

Paleontologists must be very careful when they dig for fossils. They must not break the fossils they find. They often make a map to show exactly where they find the fossils.

Imagine that you are the paleontologist who found this fossil. Use the grid to draw where you found it.

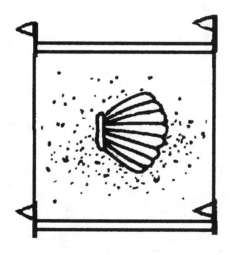
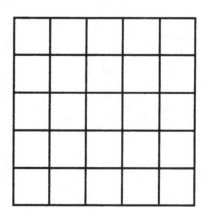

A TOOTHY GRIN

Paleontologists are able to tell what kind of food dinosaurs ate by looking at fossils of teeth. Dinosaurs that were meat eaters needed sharp teeth to pull the meat off animals they had attacked. Dinosaurs that were plant eaters needed flat, wide teeth to grind up plants.

Draw teeth on the dinosaurs below.

Meat Eaters	**Plant Eaters**

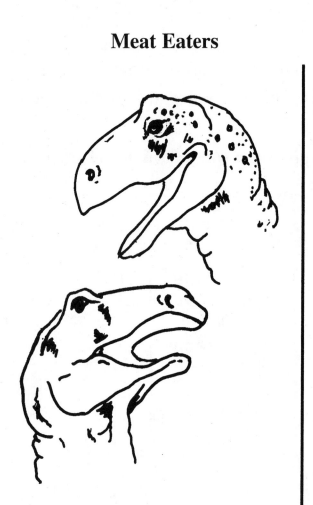
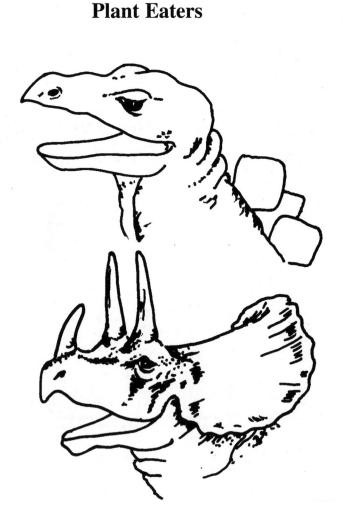

Name _____ Date _____

WHAT HAPPENED TO THE DINOSAURS?

No dinosaurs live on Earth today. They are extinct. That means that they don't exist now and that there will never be any more of them.

Some scientists think that the dinosaurs died out from diseases. Others think that the Earth was hit by an asteroid from space or that volcanoes erupted. If either of those two things happened, so much dust might have been sent into the air that the light of the Sun 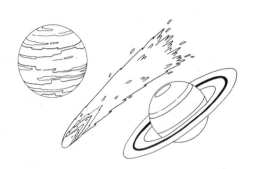 would have been blocked. That would have changed the weather. If dinosaurs or the things they ate couldn't live in the new weather, the dinosaurs would die out.

No one knows for sure why the dinosaurs became extinct. What do you think?

_____

_____

_____

_____

_____

_____

_____

_____

EXTINCT AND ENDANGERED

Dinosaurs are not the only animals that are extinct. In fact, many kinds of animals and plants become extinct every day.

Other animals and plants are **endangered.** This means that they are in danger of becoming extinct. They need special help and protection to survive.

There are many reasons why living things become extinct or endangered. Some animals are killed for their <u>meat</u>, <u>skin</u>, <u>feathers</u>, or <u>fur</u>. Some are killed for body <u>parts</u>, such as ivory tusks. Some are killed because people are <u>afraid</u> of them. Others are killed by <u>accident</u>.

1. _____

2. _____

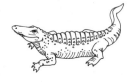

3. _____

Under the pictures, write why you think the animal is endangered. Use the underlined words.

DISAPPEARING ACT

Giant pandas are endangered animals. There are only about 900 of them left. They live in the mountain forests of China.

Pandas are plant eaters. Their favorite food is bamboo. They eat from 22 to 44 pounds (10 to 20 kilograms) of bamboo every day. It takes them about 14 hours a day just to eat!

People used to hunt pandas for their fur. Now there are laws against this. But pandas are still in danger because they can't find enough bamboo to eat. Many of the bamboo forests have been cut down to make way for houses and fields.

People are trying to help keep pandas alive. They have made special parks where pandas can come to get extra bamboo.

Draw and color a habitat for this giant panda.

Name _____ Date _____

HOW CAN WE SAVE THE ANIMALS?

Many people all over the world are trying to save endangered animals. To do this, people have to make a plan. The plan is different for each kind of animal. People find out why the animal is in trouble and then do what they can do to help. They know that all living things are important to every other living thing on our planet.

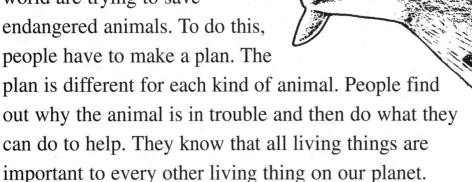

Why do people need to make a different plan for saving each different kind of endangered animal?

_____

_____

_____

_____

_____

Unit 3 Science Fair Ideas

A science fair project can help you to understand the world around you better. Choose a topic that interests you. Then use the scientific method to develop your project. Here is an example:

1. **PROBLEM:** How can a snake swallow something larger than the snake itself?

2. **HYPOTHESIS:** By researching the snake, we can find out about its special jaw that allows it to eat animals larger than itself.

3. **EXPERIMENTATION:** Research snakes to see what and how they eat. Read and watch programs about snakes. Talk to pet shop workers about snakes and observe the snakes.

4. **OBSERVATION:** Snakes have a special jaw design that allows them to open their mouths very wide. The jaws are fastened together by ligaments that can stretch a great deal. The lower jaw can drop so far down that a snake can swallow an animal up to four times larger than the snake.

5. **CONCLUSION:** By researching the snake, we find that it has a specialized jaw made for swallowing large prey.

6. **COMPARISON:** Conclusion agrees with hypothesis.

7. **PRESENTATION:** Make a poster to show pictures of different types of snakes, what they eat, and how they kill their prey. Show how the snake's jaw is different from other animals' jaws. Display a snake, if possible.

8. **RESOURCES:** Tell of any reading you did to help you with your experiment. Tell who helped you to get materials or set up your experiment.

Other Project Ideas

1. Which animals are herbivores, carnivores, and omnivores?
2. How can you demonstrate the life cycle of an amphibian?
3. How do different types of animals feed their young?
4. How do cold-blooded and warm-blooded animals react differently to temperature changes?

Healthy Bodies

Health for children revolves around healthy foods, plenty of exercise, and good hygiene. As children grow, they should begin to recognize that they can make choices that will help them live healthy lives. They need to learn the connections between what they eat and the way they look and feel. They need to have the basic information that will help them to make good food choices. Children need to know that it is never too early to begin healthy habits in eating, exercise, and hygiene. The habits they form now will affect their lives for many years to come.

Nutrition

The body needs to receive certain nutrients in order to grow and to stay healthy. These nutrients are broken down into six types: carbohydrates, protein, fat, vitamins, minerals, and water.

- Carbohydrates are sugars and starches. Sugars, such as fruits and honey, give the body quick energy while the starches, such as bread, cereal, and rice, give the body stored energy.
- Proteins come from foods such as milk, cheese, lean meat, fish, peas, and beans, and they help the body to repair itself. Proteins are used by the body to build muscle and bone, and they give the body energy.
- Fat is important for energy, too, and it helps to keep the body warm, but if the body does not use the fats put into it, it will store the fat. Fats come from foods such as meat, milk, butter, oil, and nuts.
- Vitamins are important to the body in many ways. Vitamins help the other nutrients in a person's body work together. Lack of certain vitamins can cause serious illnesses. Vitamin A, for example, which is found in foods such as broccoli, carrots, radishes, and liver, helps with eyesight. Vitamin B, from green leafy vegetables, eggs, and milk, helps with growth and energy. Vitamin C, from citrus fruits, cauliflower, strawberries, tomatoes, peppers, and broccoli, prevents sickness.
- Milk, vegetables, liver, seafood, and raisins are some of the foods that provide the minerals necessary for growth. Calcium is a mineral that helps build strong bones, and iron is needed for healthy red blood.
- Water makes up most of the human body and helps to keep our temperature normal. It is healthy and recommended to drink several glasses of water each day.

Foods have long been divided into four basic food groups—meat, milk, vegetable-fruit, and bread-cereal. New discoveries have led to a change in the divisions so that in a food pyramid, fruits and vegetables are separated, and fats are included at the top of the pyramid. The recommended servings for each group have also changed over time. Eating the right amount of foods from each group each day gives one a balanced diet. Eating too many foods from one group or not enough of another group can lead to deficiencies or weight problems. Although vitamin supplements can help with these deficiencies, vitamins are best absorbed in the body naturally through the digestion of the foods that contain them.

- The Bread-Cereal (Grain) Group contains foods made from grains such as wheat, corn, rice, oats, and barley. Six to eleven servings from this group each day give you carbohydrates, vitamins, and minerals.

- The Vegetable Group and the Fruit Group contain vitamins, minerals, and carbohydrates. Two to four servings of fruits and three to five servings of vegetables each day are recommended.

- <u>The Meat Group</u> includes chicken, fish, red meats, peas, nuts, and eggs. The meat group contains much of the protein we get from our diets, but it also includes fats. Two to three servings from the meat group each day are recommended.

- <u>The Milk Group</u> includes milk (whole and skim), butter, cheese, yogurt, and ice cream and gives us fat, vitamins, protein, and minerals that are important for strong bones and teeth, such as Vitamin D. Two to three servings from the milk group each day are recommended.

- <u>The Fats, Oils, and Sweets</u> group, including butter, oil, and margarine, should be eaten sparingly.

Hygiene

Keeping the body clean is an important part of staying healthy. Children need to know that when they wash, they are washing off viruses and bacteria, or germs, which can cause illness. Washing the hair and body regularly prevents bacteria from entering the skin through cuts and from getting into the mouth. Hands should always be washed after handling garbage or using the bathroom.

Germs can also come from other people. Children should be discouraged from sharing straws, cups, or other utensils. They should be reminded always to cover their mouths when they sneeze or cough, and to use tissue frequently. Children also need to be reminded not to share combs or hats.

Teeth

Regular brushing and flossing can help keep teeth healthy. Avoiding sweets also helps. Most children have all their baby teeth by the time they are two years old. When they are about seven, they begin to lose their baby teeth, and permanent teeth begin to appear. Although the baby teeth will fall out, it is important to take good care of them and the gums that surround them.

Exercise and Sleep

Muscles grow when they are used and contract when they are not used. Muscles that become unaccustomed to exercise can be injured by sudden or strenuous activity. This is why muscles should be exercised regularly and in moderation. Occasional strenuous activity is not advantageous to the muscles and does not give long-term results. Exercising the muscles makes the body grow larger and stronger and helps make the heart strong.

Regular exercise can relax the body and help people get a good night's rest. Sleep is an important part of keeping the body healthy. People need different amounts of sleep at different times of their lives. Babies sleep most of the time because their bodies are growing very quickly. School children usually require from eight to ten hours of sleep, and adults need about seven or eight hours daily. Sleep allows the body and mind to rest. If we don't get enough sleep, our bodies and minds do not function as well as they should. Our attention wanders and we become forgetful. Our muscles will feel weak and less coordinated. Lack of sleep can also make people irritable and impair their judgment.

The Five Senses and the Nervous System

The human body collects information using the five senses—sight, smell, hearing, taste, and touch. The nervous system enables us to put all of our senses together so that messages are sent to the brain and we are able to act according to the information that the brain receives. The nervous system enables us to react. It controls all of the other systems in the body.

The major organ of the nervous system is the brain. Another part of the nervous system is a system of nerves that carry information to the brain. The third part of the nervous system is the sense organs. The nose is the sense organ for the sense of smell. There are many nerve cells in the nose that take the information regarding odors to a main nerve called the olfactory nerve. The olfactory nerve carries the information to your brain. Your brain will then tell your body what to do with the information.

Safety

Children need to take part in ensuring their own safety. They need to be provided with the information necessary to stay safe as they do more and more on their own. Basic safety rules for water, fire, and thunderstorms are reviewed in this unit. Children should also be aware of basic bicycle safety rules. Class discussions about these important safety rules should be conducted. Students should be encouraged to discuss why the rules are important and the consequences of not following the rules.

Name _____ Date _____

EATING WELL

To be healthy, you need many different foods.

Color the foods in each group.

Do you eat the right number of servings from each group?

Vegetables and Fruits

Eat four servings each day.

Bread and Cereal

Eat four servings each day.

Meat and Beans

Eat two servings each day.

Milk

Eat two servings each day.

© Steck-Vaughn Company

Unit 4: Health and Safety
Life Science 2, SV 3842-5

Name _____ Date _____

WHAT DO YOU EAT IN ONE DAY?

Carry this chart with you for one day.
Write down what you eat.

	Vegetable-Fruit Group	Bread-Cereal Group	Meat-Bean Group	Milk Group
Breakfast				
Lunch				
Dinner				
Snacks				

Name _____ Date _____

HOW WE GET ENERGY

Read each sentence.
Which word makes the sentence true?
Circle the letter of the correct answer.

1. We get _____ from food.
   a. energy   **b.** work   **c.** sick

2. Your body uses food as _____.
   a. play   **b.** fuel   **c.** rest

3. We need food to stay _____.
   a. hungry   **b.** sick   **c.** healthy

4. We also need _____ to stay healthy.
   a. fuel   **b.** sleep   **c.** hunger

Name _____ Date _____

TRAIL MIX

This snack tastes good.

It is also good for you.

You can take it along to eat when you go hiking.

Trail Mix Recipe

Get a small plastic bag.

Put a little of each of these in the bag:

> peanuts
>
> raisins
>
> walnuts
>
> coconut
>
> any other nuts or dried fruit you like.

Close the bag and shake.

Enjoy!

Unit 4: Health and Safety
Life Science 2, SV 3842-5

Name _____   Date _____

HOW WE USE ENERGY

Look at each picture.
Write *yes* under the things that take a lot of energy.
Write *no* under the things that do not take a lot of energy.

1. _____

2. _____

3. _____

4. _____

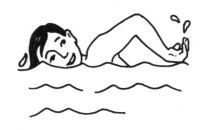

5. _____

6. _____

7. We need _____ to work and play.

© Steck-Vaughn Company

Unit 4: Health and Safety
Life Science 2, SV 3842-5

Name _____ Date _____

STAYING HEALTHY

Look at the pictures.
Complete each sentence.

1. W_____ every day.

2. Brush your t_____.

3. Eat good f_____.

4. Go to b_____ early.

Unit 4: **Health and Safety**
Life Science 2, SV 3842-5

OUR FIVE SENSES

We learn about the world by seeing.
We can also learn by hearing, smelling, tasting, and touching.

How do we learn about these things?
Draw lines to show.

1. 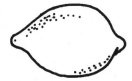 see

2.  hear

3.  smell

4.   taste

5.  touch

Unit 4: Health and Safety
Life Science 2, SV 3842-5

MY SCIENCE OBSERVATION

This morning, I tasted _____

_____

_____.

On my way to school, I saw_____

_____

_____.

In school, I heard _____

_____

_____.

After school, I tasted _____

_____

_____.

At bedtime, I felt _____

_____

_____.

TAKE CARE OF YOUR EARS

Which things are good for your ears?
Color them.

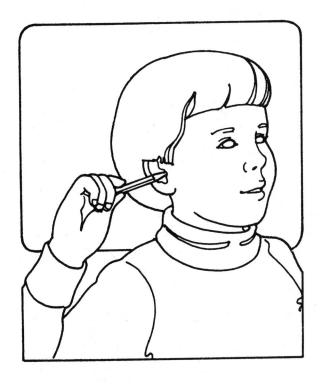
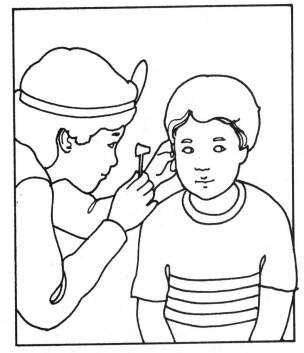
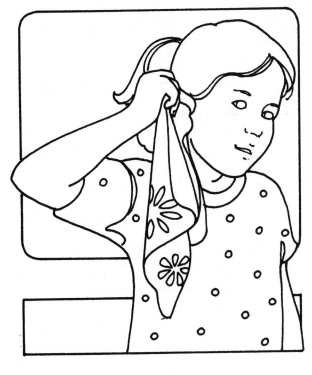
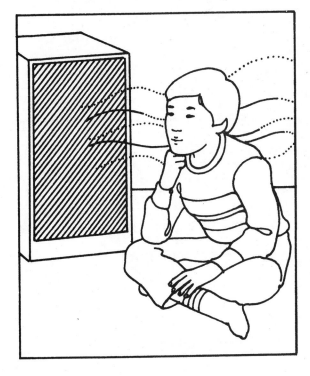

ARE TWO EARS BETTER THAN ONE?

You need a partner to do this.

Blindfold your partner.

Stand about ten feet away.

Hit two pencils together.

Your partner should point to the

direction of the sound.

Be very quiet and change positions.

Hit the pencils together again.

Take ten different positions.

How many times was your partner right? _____

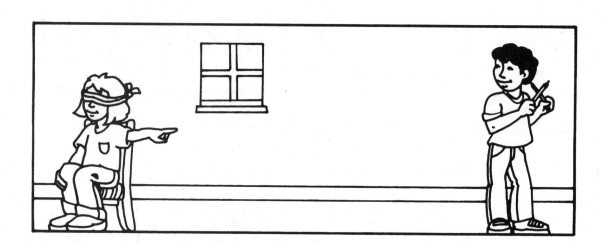

Have your partner plug one ear.

Take ten positions again.

How many times was your partner right this time? _____

Are two ears better than one? _____

ARE TWO EYES BETTER THAN ONE?

How well do you play catch?

Get a small ball.

Play catch with a friend.

Stand about 15 feet apart.

You get ten chances.

How many times did you

catch the ball? _____

Now cover one eye.

You get another ten chances.

How many times did you catch the ball? _____

Are two eyes better than one? _____

Your Heart and Lungs

Your heart and lungs are important organs.
Do you know where they are?

Do This

A. From a roll of paper, cut a piece long enough to lie down on.

B. Have a friend trace your body on the paper.

C. Draw in your heart.
It is about the size of your fist.

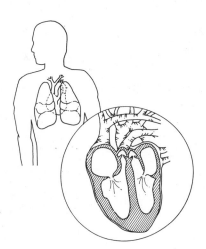

D. Draw in your lungs.
Each lung is about the size of your open hand.

E. Draw in your sense organs, too!

116

Name _____ Date _____

A CHECKUP

Draw lines from the pictures to the right sentences.

1. The doctor checks your ears.

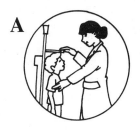

2. The doctor measures your height and weight.

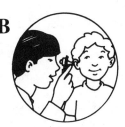

3. The doctor looks at your throat.

4. The doctor checks your eyes.

5. The doctor listens to your heart.

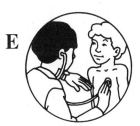

Unit 4: Health and Safety
Life Science 2, SV 3842-5

Do You Take Good Care of Yourself?

Do you take good care of yourself?
Take this test.
Check *Yes* or *No* for each question.

	Yes	No
1. I eat many different kinds of foods.		
2. I get enough sleep every night.		
3. I wash my hands before I eat.		
4. I brush my teeth every morning and night.		
5. I visit the dentist at least once a year.		
6. I run around and play each day.		
7. I don't eat a lot of candy and other sweets.		
8. I wear warm clothes when it is cold outside.		

Did you answer *Yes* to every question?

If so, then you do take good care of yourself. Draw a picture of yourself
doing each of these things.

WHAT TO DO ABOUT INSECT PESTS

1. Keep cool and bathe often.
2. Do not wear perfume.
3. Do not wear bright colors or flowers.
4. Wear long sleeves and pants in the evenings.
5. Do not walk barefoot outside.
6. Use an insect repellent.
7. Do not swat at bees. Move away slowly.
8. Do not leave picnic food out.

Look at the picture.
Circle what is wrong.
Write the number of the rule being broken.

Unit 4: Health and Safety
Life Science 2, SV 3842-5

Name _____ Date _____

POISON IVY

Do you know what poison ivy looks like?
Here is a hint:

Leaves of three, let them be!

The leaves have an oil on them.
The oil causes a rash.
Find a picture of poison ivy.
Draw it here.

THUNDERSTORM SAFETY

Go over these rules with your family.

Then quiz each other. For example, ask, "What would you do if you were on the phone when a thunderstorm started?"

Thunderstorm Safety Rules

1. Stay indoors.
2. Stay away from open windows.
3. Do not talk on the phone.
4. If you cannot get inside, do not go under a tall tree. Try to get into thick woods.
5. Stay away from metal objects.
6. Get out of and away from water.
7. If you are in an open area, get down on your knees. Put your hands on your knees. Tuck your head.

Name _____   Date _____

FIRE SAFETY

Do you know what to do in case of fire?
Here are some fire safety rules.
Unscramble the words in each sentence.

> **Stop,
> Drop,
> and Roll!**

1. Keep ___ ___ ___ ___ .
    M   C   A   L

2. ___ ___ ___ ___ everyone in the building about the fire.
    N   A   W   R

3. Get ___ ___ ___ of the burning building.
    T   U   O

4. Be ___ ___ ___ ___ ___ ___ ___ when you leave the building.
    F   U   L   R   E   C   A

    Do not open doors that are ___ ___ ___ .
    T   O   H

    Try to find another way ___ ___ ___ .
    U   O   T

5. Call the ___ ___ ___ ___ department.
    I   R   F   E

6. Do not go back ___ ___ ___ ___ ___ ___ the building.
    S   I   I   N   E   D

7. If your clothes catch fire, ___ ___ ___ ___ moving.
    O   T   S   P

    ___ ___ ___ ___ to the floor. Cover your face and ___ ___ ___ ___ .
    R   O   P   D   L   O   R   L

WATER SAFETY RULES

Unscramble the words in these rules.

1. __ __ __ __ __ how to swim.

   E   R   L   N   A

2. Always __ __ __ __ with someone.

   M   I   W   S

3. Swim only where a lifeguard is __ __ __ __ __ __ __ __.

   T   C   I   A   W   G   H   N

4. Never call for __ __ __ __ unless you really need help.

   E   P   H   L

5. Swim only in water that is __ __ __ __ for swimming.

   A   F   S   E

6. When boating, always wear a __ __ __ __ jacket.

   F   I   E   L

7. Do not __ __ __ __ into water if you do not know the depth.

   I   D   V   E

Unit 4: Health and Safety
Life Science 2, SV 3842-5

Name _____ Date _____

BICYCLE SAFETY RULES

1. Ride on the right-hand side of the street.
2. Obey all traffic signs.
3. Use hand signals.
4. Have a light on your bicycle if you ride at night.
   Wear light-colored clothing.

Are these children following bicycle safety rules?
Circle those who are.
Put an X on those who are not.

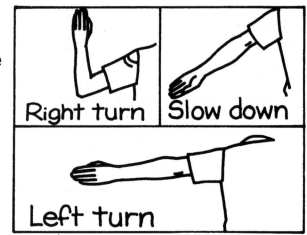

Right turn | Slow down

Left turn

Unit 4: **Health and Safety**
Life Science 2, SV 3842-5

WHY SHOULD YOU HAVE REFLECTORS ON YOUR BICYCLE?

Materials:
- red and black construction paper • scissors • silver glitter • glue
- flashlight • bicycle reflectors • newspaper

Do This

A. Draw two shapes on red paper. Cut out the shapes.

B. Put small dots of glue on one shape.

C. Sprinkle silver glitter on the glue.

D. Place both shapes on a piece of black paper.

E. Turn off the lights. Shine a flashlight on the shapes.

What do you see?

1. Which shape is easier to see?

   _____

What do you think?

2. Which shape is like a bicycle reflector?

   _____

3. How can bicycle reflectors help keep you safe at night?

   _____

Unit 4: Health and Safety
Life Science 2, SV 3842-5

Name _____ Date _____

Unit 4 Science Fair Ideas

A science fair project can help you to understand the world around you better. Choose a topic that interests you. Then use the scientific method to develop your project. Here is an example:

1. **PROBLEM:** How do our bodies use energy?
2. **HYPOTHESIS:** Our bodies use energy at different levels all of the time.
3. **EXPERIMENTATION:** Think about what you do each day. Watch what the people in your family do during the day. Watch what your classmates do. Decide which activities require energy. Which activities require the most energy? the least?
4. **OBSERVATION:** Everything we do requires energy. Some things require more energy than others do. Sleeping, reading, and playing quietly do not require a lot of energy. Playing hard and working hard require a lot of energy.
5. **CONCLUSION:** Our bodies use energy at different levels all of the time.
6. **COMPARISON:** Conclusion agrees with hypothesis.
7. **PRESENTATION:** Make posters showing activities that require large amounts of energy and those that require less energy. Cut out pictures from magazines of activities that require different levels of energy. Paste them on your posters. Do a high-level activity like running in place. Then do a low-level activity like sitting and reading. Show the difference between the activities.
8. **RESOURCES:** Tell of any reading you did to help you with your experiment. Tell who helped you to get materials or set up your experiment.

Other Project Ideas

1. How do your senses help you to learn about what is going on around you?
2. Can some foods hurt our bodies?
3. What happens if people do not get enough sleep?
4. Why is it important to know safety rules?

Life Science
Grade Two
Answer Key

P. 9 Unit 1 Assessment: 1. b 2. a 3. c 4. desert 5. rain forest 6. food, shelter, air, water 7. Plants produce oxygen, and they are the food for planteaters, which are the food for meateaters. 8. It destroys, or harms, them.

P. 10 Unit 2 Assessment: A. 1. roots 2. Water, stem 3. leaves 4. sunlight, food 5. Fungi 6. Seeds 7. Tree 8. needles 9. soil B. Students draw a flower showing the roots, stem, and leaves. They label the leaves a, the stem b, the roots c, and the flower's blossom d.

P. 11 Unit 3 Assessment: A. Chart answers given left to right for each row: Mammal/has fur, soft/walks/live babies/hamster; Reptile/hard, dry scales/slithers/lays eggs/lizard; Amphibian/smooth, wet skin/hops or crawls/eggs in water/frog; Fish/has scales/swims/eggs in water/salmon; Bird/feathers/flies/eggs in nests/robin; Insect/hard body, or 3-parts, or exoskeleton/crawls/eggs/ant B. Drawings will vary. C. 1. They find and observe fossils. 2. Possible answers include: killed for its meat, skin, feathers, fur, or body parts; killed by accident; killed because people are afraid of them; changes in its environment.

P. 12 Unit 4 Assessment: A. 1. energy 2. foods 3. rest 4. safe 5. alone 6. teeth 7. bicycle 8. burning 9. inside 10. street B. Answers may vary. 11. d 12. a 13. b 14. e 15. c

P. 15 Students should draw a line from the squirrel to the woods, from the seal to the ocean, from the kangaroo rat to the desert, and from the monkey to the rain forest.

P. 16 In any order: 1. food 2. water 3. air 4. shelter

P. 17 Students color the spider, ladybug, squirrel, bird, butterfly, and rabbit; students circle the worm, mole, and ants.

P. 18 Students draw worms in the tunnels; should show dead plants that they are eating.

P. 19 1. dry 2. wet

P. 20 Students mark X on the monkey, the squirrel, the toucan, and the owl.

P. 21 Students color all three cacti.

P. 23 Students circle 1, 3, 4, 5

P. 24 Students circle the plant, the soil, and/or the Sun.

P. 25 Drawings will vary.

P. 26 Check students' drawings for a sea creature that cannot live in fresh water, such as a shark, whale, shrimp, lobster, kelp, etc.

P. 27 Students should mark an X on 1. mouth 2. stingers 3. stingers 4. claws 5. tentacles 6. claws 7. tentacles

P. 28 [Picture order: 2, 3, 1, 4] 1. They would die. 2. They would die. 3. No, there would not be any fish. 4. All living things depend on plants because they eat the plants or they eat animals that eat plants.

P. 29 2. These animals live in the forest because it has all the things they need to live; clean water, food, shelter (such as the cave and the trees), and clean air.

P. 30 Students should circle the trash on the ground near the picnic table and near the bottom of the picture and they should circle the tire in the water.

P. 31 Students should draw an empty can in the Metal bin, and a newspaper in the Paper bin.

P. 32 1. E 2. D 3. C 4. B, A 5. C

P. 36 Check students' drawings for correct labeling of roots, stems, and leaves.

P. 37 taproot: long, thick; fibrous roots: short, thin

P. 38 1. The potato grew small roots. The inside of the potato turned reddish in color. 2. The potato changed because it was placed in water. It grew roots that absorbed some of the water.

P. 39 Students draw arrows from the tips of the roots up to the blossom of the plant and to the leaves.

P. 40 1. The leaves turned a reddish color. 2. The tiny tubes of the stalk had red water in them. 3. Water travels up through the stem to the leaves of a plant.

P. 42 Students' drawings will vary.

P. 43 Students should draw the Sun and water and/or air.

P. 44 1. Drops of water formed on the inside of the jar. 2. The water came from the leaves of the plant.

P. 45 Students' drawings will vary.

P. 46 In any order, students should draw soil, water, air, and Sun.

P. 47 1. The seeds in the warm place grew faster because cold temperature slows seed growth. 2. Warm weather is best for seeds to grow. This is why seeds sprout and grow in the spring and not in the winter.

P. 48 1. Possible groupings may include: fruits, vegetables, flowers, nuts, and tree seeds. 2. Answers will vary depending on how the students grouped the seeds. 3. The students may note differences in size, shape, color, texture, hardness, and whether the seeds are edible.

P. 49 Students should circle the popcorn, peanuts, peanut butter, wheat (bread), peas, and beans.

P. 51 Yes, seeds would grow well in potting soil because potting soil is a mixture of sand and clay; therefore, the roots can spread out and the soil will hold water.

P. 52 Drawings will vary.

P. 53 Dates will vary.

P. 54 1. The houseplant's leaves are frozen and wilted. The evergreen leaves are alive. 2. No. 3. Yes.

P. 55 1. Both leaves are limp and yellowish-brown. 2. Plants need air. The leaf that was covered with a plastic bag did not receive air and is not healthy. 3. Plants need sunlight. Sunlight keeps the leaves green and healthy. Plants need sunlight in order to make food.

P. 56 1. plants 2. salt 3. float 4. shallow 5. microscope 6. sunlight 7. colors

P. 57 1. The plants do not look the same. The land plants are mostly green. Water plants can be many different colors. Land plants have roots, stems, and leaves. Water plants often do not have roots. 2. Water plants feel slippery or slimy; they are usually very limp. Land plants feel dry. They are stiff and can stand upright 3. They do not smell the same. The individual smells will vary depending upon the plants used in the activity. 4. You can tell whether a plant lives in water or on land by looking at its colors, whether it has roots, and if it is stiff and dry or slimy and limp.

P. 58 Seeds: peas, beans; Stems: celery stalks, asparagus; Flowers: broccoli florets, cauliflower; Roots: carrots, radishes

P. 59 1. Mold is growing on the bread and the apple. The mold looks fuzzy and is many different colors. 2. Mold is alive. 3. Mold is alive because it feeds on the apple and bread and grows larger each day.

P. 60 Check students' work.

P. 61 Drawings will vary. Check if it is labeled correctly.

P. 62 Students should draw a line from 1. to the needles and cone, and from 2. to the leaves and acorns. The mushrooms and ferns (3. and 4.) live in the forest and should be colored.

P. 63 Algae: This is plant-like but has no roots, stems, or flowers. This plant-like living thing lives in water.; Fungi: This living thing cannot make its own food. This living thing can grow on dead plants and animals.; Moss: This green plant grows in damp, shady places. This green plant feels like a soft rug and has no flowers.

P. 69 1. no 2. yes 3. yes 4. yes

P. 70 Drawings will vary. 1. Teeth should be flat and wide for chewing. 2. Teeth should be sharp and pointed for tearing.

P. 71 Students should color the elephant's ears and trunk. (They may color the entire elephant since the whole elephant is mentioned in the text.)

P. 72 DOWN: 1. fur 3. alive 4. milk ACROSS: 2. warm 5. lungs 6. babies

P. 73 1.-3. Answers will vary. 4. No, all mammals do not eat the same things.

P. 74 A. a. mouth b. fin c. gills d. scales, B. Scales help protect the fish. Gills help the fish breathe. Fins help the fish move. Mouth helps the fish eat. C. 1. - 6. Answers will vary.

P. 75 Students should color all animals but the dolphin.

P. 76 Students should color the 2 fish at the top of the tank blue and the 2 fish at the bottom of the tank yellow.

P. 77 1. The scales look like hard plates that overlap. 2. The gills are found inside slits in the fish's body; they feel soft and thin. 3. The fins look like fans. They can be easily moved. They feel soft in the middle and a bit stiffer around the edges. 4. The scales are hard so they protect the fish's body from injury. 5. The gills are thin so air in the water can pass through them. 6. The fins move easily so they can be used to steer the fish through the water.

P. 78 1.-4. Answers will vary depending upon the animals chosen.

P. 80 1. The birds ate 2 raisins, 8 seeds, 0 crackers, and 3 peanuts. 2. seeds

P. 81 1. The water rolled off the feathers instead of soaking into the feathers. 2. Birds do not get wet when it rains because the oil in their feathers sheds water so the rain never reaches the bird's body. 3. Feathers help birds to stay warm; feathers form a smooth surface that reduces air friction and helps birds to fly; tail feathers help birds to steer in flight.

P. 83 1. no 2. no 3. no

Life Science
Grade Two
Answer Key

P. 84   1. Answers will vary depending upon the groups identified by the students. 2. The students may identify groups based on size, the way they move, body characteristics, or habitat.

P. 87   It had two legs so that it could move quickly to chase its prey. It probably had lightweight skin to keep it cool. It had sharp claws to help catch prey and sharp teeth for eating meat.

P. 88   1. a 2. c 3. b 4. egg, tadpole with gills, tadpole with legs and lungs, adult.

P. 89   1. Students' pictures should be arranged as follows: egg, tadpole with tail, tadpole with legs, adult frog. 2. Other amphibian life cycles include those of a toad and salamander.

P. 90   1. 3 2. 6 3. 2

P. 91   1. 6 2. 25

P. 93   1. 6 2. It moves by flying, crawling, or hopping. 3. Students may observe that the insects have chewing mouth parts or sucking mouth parts. 4. All insects have six legs and three distinct body parts. Most have four wings.

P. 94   Dog: mammal, on land, warm-blooded, alive, fur; Bird: bird, on land, warm-blooded, hatches from eggs, feathers; Fish: fish, in water, cold-blooded, from eggs, scales; Frog: amphibian, near water, cold-blooded, from eggs, smooth; Snake: reptile, on land, cold-blooded, from eggs or alive, scales

P. 96   The meat-eating dinosaurs' teeth should be sharp and pointed. The plant-eating dinosaurs' teeth should be wide and flat.

P. 97   Answers will vary.

P. 98   Answers will vary.

P. 100   Answers will vary. A different plan is needed for each animal because each animal has a different type of problem.

P. 107   1. a 2. b 3. c 4. b

P. 109   1. no 2. yes 3. yes 4. no 5. yes 6. no 7. energy

P. 110   1. Wash 2. teeth 3. foods 4. bed

P. 111   Answers may vary. 1. lemon/taste 2. cactus/touch 3. television/see 4. rose/smell 5. radio/hear

P. 112   Students' observations will vary. Introduce this exercise to students early in the day. Discuss the kinds of things they should think about writing as they go through the day. Have students complete the exercise at home and bring it back to school for the next day's class.

P. 113   Students should color the checkup and the girl washing her ears with a cloth. The boy should not put anything in his ear. The boy near the speaker is too close.

P. 114   Answers will vary. Two ears are better than one for telling the direction of a sound.

P. 115   Answers will vary. Two eyes are better than one for judging distance and catching.

P. 117   1. B 2. A 3. D 4. C 5. E

P. 119   Students should circle the girl with flowers (rule 3), the boy with bare feet (rule 5), the boy swatting bees (rule 7), and the picnic food left out (rule 8).

P. 120   Poison ivy has leaves in groups of three, greenish flowers, and ivory-colored berries.

P. 122   1. calm 2. Warn 3. out 4. careful, hot, out 5. fire 6. inside 7. stop, drop, roll

P. 123   1. Learn 2. swim 3. watching 4. help 5. safe 6. life 7. dive

P. 124   Students should circle the girl who is signaling and the boy who has his lights on. They should put an X on the girl who is riding into traffic and the boy who is riding in traffic. Also, you should always wear a helmet when riding a bike.

P. 125   1. The shape with glitter on it is easier to see because glitter reflects the light. 2. The shape with glitter is like a bicycle reflector. 3. Bicycle reflectors can help keep you safe at night because they reflect the light from cars. This makes it easier for drivers to see the bicycle.